Self-Grooming Guide
for a PERFECT
MAN

I0031887

Prem P. Bhalla

V&S PUBLISHERS

Published by:

V&S PUBLISHERS

F-2/16, Ansari Road, Daryaganj, New Delhi-110002
011-23240026, 011-23240027 • *Fax:* 011-23240028
Email: info@vspublishers.com • *Website:* www.vspublishers.com

Branch : Hyderabad
5-1-707/1, Brij Bhawan (Beside Central Bank of India Lane)
Bank Street, Koti, Hyderabad - 500 095
040-24737290
E-mail: vspublishershyd@gmail.com

Follow us on:

For any assistance sms **VSPUB** to **56161**
All books available at **www.vspublishers.com**

Previously Published as : The Portrait of a Complete Man
© Copyright: Author
ISBN 978-93-813844-7-3
Edition 2013

Printed at : Param Offseters, Okhla, New Delhi-110020

Author's Note

I like reading jokes. I think everybody does. We enjoy some readily. Occasionally we come across one that not only refreshes us, but also sets the mind thinking. I read one more than two decades ago and I still keep thinking about it. I do not know how many times I must have repeated it. It was not an anecdote. It was a definition – of a specialist. It said a specialist is a person who knows more and more about less and less until he knows everything about nothing! How true!

In our scramble for power through specialised knowledge, to qualify for special positions, modern man is proving the definition true. In pursuit of this specialised knowledge, modern man has gone to such extremes that he has achieved what he set out to, but has lost the balance of living. He has forgotten the very purpose for which he joined the race. We find specialists in every sphere of life. They occupy special positions. They are admired. However, they are incomplete individuals, with much knowledge about their field, but none about life and living.

To be progressive in life, it is not enough to be a specialist. The world needs "the complete man". We need individuals who live a complete life for themselves, for their families, and for the communities they live in. Is this possible? Of course, it is. God has blessed everyone to live a complete life. The rest depends upon the individual.

The Portrait of a Complete Man strives to guide one to live a balanced life, a complete life. Read it. Think about what you read. Re-read portions that appeal to you. Adapt what appears useful to you. Be happy. Succeed at your work. Have a happy home. Bring up happy children. Contribute to the society that has given you so much. As you enjoy the benefits of a balanced life, you become "the complete man".

INTRODUCTION

A man's place in society depends upon the image he projects of himself. In the hope of achieving good results, most people go to great lengths to win the approval of people who matter to them. It is this desire for appreciation that compels people to dress to attract attention, to build and decorate their homes in a style which may not necessarily reflect the comfort they derive from them, to acquire status symbols like luxury cars, air-conditioners, television sets, imported household appliances, and other articles. These possessions can single them out amongst others.

However, little do these people realise that they have entered a never-ending race. It is a race nobody can possibly win. Like them, there are many that, irrespective of the pleasure they may derive from their possessions, follow a similar pattern. They try to impress others without a thought as to where it would finally end.

What do people think of you? Perhaps different people have varied opinions. Your wife and the family who know you intimately may have one impression about you and friends quite another. It is possible that people in general will have yet another opinion about you. In addition, what may appear stranger is that you may think very differently about yourself, thus creating many separate images of yourself.

Each one of us is many persons in one. Most people are content as they are. Nevertheless, not the complete man. Such a man sees a purpose in life. To get ahead, he wants to make the best of nature's gifts. He is conscientious, honest and straightforward. He constantly endeavours to remove the parallax between the several images that he may cast in his everyday life.

Although different people may interpret his words and deeds to suit their personal convenience, yet the fault may lie in his own erratic actions. To ensure it is not so, he often reviews and amends his actions to project a fair image of himself. He creates harmony between his actions and the image he wants to project of himself. He must understand the many factors that affect this image. Also, how he can exercise the maximum control over them to gain personal advantage.

Why does a man behave as he does? We are what our basic characteristics, as inherited from our parents, have made us when they reacted with the environments in which we have grown up and are presently living in. Living is a continuous process. Change is an integral part of our life. Each day, every hour and every minute, our life is undergoing a change. Whether it is for the better or for worse depends upon how we react to the environment. Since no two people have the same inherited characteristics, each one reacts differently to similar environments and grows up to be an individual personality, unique in every way.

Life is a continuous struggle for existence. Only the fittest can make a mark in life. However frail and innocent a baby may appear, he too learns to cope with the environments that surround him. He has his own methods to draw attention to and fulfil his needs. Since it is not possible to have all of one's desires fulfilled the way one wishes, it becomes necessary to compromise with certain aspects of life. This is not without some anxiety and tension within us. How we cope with this anxiety and tension influences the habits and attitudes that eventually become a part of us.

Each person, in keeping with his basic nature

inherited from parents, adopts a particular way of living to cope with anxieties and tensions. Some become men of action, doers rather than thinkers. However, many may find peace in being alone. They are planners rather than executors. Others may avoid tension by seeking perfection in everything. Some may prefer to be emotional or dramatic. We cannot ignore the weaker ones who may become suspicious, or those who may lean upon imaginary ailments to cope with the anxieties of living.

At the outset, some of these ways of livings may appear attractive and some even unpleasant. However, none of these is forever impressive, or useful, if found in the extreme form. Fortunately, most of us are a mixture of different types, with one type predominating. This makes it necessary that everyone must understand himself. One should develop those habits and attitudes that are useful in the given circumstances. In the beginning, this may seem difficult, but it is possible through learning, through a deliberate effort in the right direction.

For the complete man, the best rule is to do what comes naturally. Do not try to do things that are contrary to your basic nature. If you prefer your own company rather than being at a loud party, do not let it hurt your conscience. In the same way, if you are a man of action, it will do you no good if you decide to do something that requires a lot of thinking. Living unnaturally cannot be disguised. It will only promote tension. Therefore, the secret of success really lies in developing that which you can do effortlessly and in trying to eliminate what makes you tense and uneasy.

To be accepted in life as a complete man, it is not enough that you discipline yourself only. You are undoubtedly the most important component in the set-up. However, you cannot expect to be appreciated until you make a positive effort to influence or recondition the people and the environment around you. This is not easy. People have spent their entire lifetime in improving their own techniques to achieve this objective. One can take advantage of the knowledge passed down from generation to generation, but what is required is wisdom, and this grows only from within, through patience and perseverance.

Many people are in search of a formula for creating a good image instantly. It is true that some film stars, sportsmen and political figures gain the limelight overnight. However, it can be deceptive. Even when the limelight does fall on them, it only covers a certain sphere of their activities and not the whole. They may get public appreciation and recognition, and rightly so too, as their success may be built upon talent and years of hard work. Nevertheless, we cannot ignore the other aspects of life. A happy life envisages an all-round development. It is not enough that one should achieve success in one's profession or in a special activity. The complete man is interested in an all-round development whereby he can fulfil all his natural desires. Besides success at work, he looks forward to harmony at home and pleasant relationships with his family members and friends.

A good public image is not made up of a single act of great merit. Nor does it consist in possessing more material benefits than what others possess. It is the sum of the total effect created by the individual's thoughts, actions, habits, attitudes and personal philosophies. One's education, competence in business or profession, a pleasant home life, efficiency in meeting the challenges of the day and many other factors affect the personal image. Few people can really manage to create a fair balance between these factors, but the sum total effect can be very interesting.

Men who have brought about progress have not reached high positions through sheer luck. Nature has provided equal opportunities to everyone. Complete men make continuous self-improvement their primary target. By periodically reviewing their experiences gained through the application of knowledge, they have adjusted

CONTENTS

SECTION—I

DISCOVERING YOURSELF

Discover yourself. Deep within you is a new and better individual, a personality radiating greater magnetism waiting to emerge. Eternal happiness is awaiting you. Yet, most of us are obsessed with our bodies and forever worried about our health. Am I normal? Is my health all right? Do I need extra care or attention?

Nineteen out of twenty times, there is nothing wrong with us. Even if there were, we need to remember a simple truth. Every problem has a solution. Many of these are very simple and within our control. We only need to understand ourselves better and view our problems in the correct perspective. Right before us, we have a solution.

Discover yourself. Begin by understanding the hidden meanings of your own desires in life. Nobody can understand them better than you can. To realise these you will need strength. There could be no better source of knowledge and power than the great storehouse of nature. It bestows its benefits to everyone who can learn to live in harmony with himself and his environment. You can draw abundantly on this great storehouse through self-discipline. Live as close to nature as possible. It will give you strength of character, good health and inner peace.

The greatest of all needs is peace of mind. Without it, life would be hell. Yet, many have to do without it because they do not desire or work for it earnestly. They only wish for it. They expect this need to be fulfilled through divine blessing. Before happiness can become an integral part of you, the desire to be happy should be a part of you. As the desire sinks into the subconscious mind, energy is released to spur one into action. The determination to gain it conditions the actions to become useful habits. It is not long before the goal is within easy reach.

1. Finding Happiness

> "Happiness can be built only on virtue, and must of necessity, have truth for its foundation."
>
> —Coleridge

All human efforts are directed to achieve a common goal: personal happiness!

The struggle to turn this dream into reality begins in early childhood. These years are spent in preparing ourselves to face the challenges of adult life and to equip ourselves with the knowledge that can help us make happiness a constant companion. We put in our best efforts to move towards our goal. Except for the blessed few that attain it, the goal eludes the rest. Disheartened, many resign themselves to their defeat, accepting it as part of their destiny. However, with a few rays of hope still burning bright, some sustain the struggle until they reach their goal, or time runs out on them.

Considering the circumstances, the complete man pauses to question whether eternal happiness is really the prerogative of a blessed few. Could it not become a part of everyone's life? If so, how can it be done? What special qualities are required in a man to achieve this state?

The answer is simple. Happiness is for everyone. If we have failed to make it a part of our life, then each individual is to blame for his shortcomings. We only need to understand the meaning of true happiness. By cultivating the habits that promote it, one can effortlessly live an eternally happy life.

What is Happiness?

What does happiness mean to you? Good health? Harmony at home? Lots of money? Alternatively, perhaps something similar? All these things do give some happiness to a person. Yet, one needs to understand the difference between transient happiness and that which becomes a part of oneself.

Transient happiness comes from feeding the senses with continuous thrills and excitement. Although it may be very pleasurable at that time, it is temporary and fades away when the senses are not exposed to newer thrills. Unchecked indulgence in this form of pleasure or happiness can eventually affect one's personal values in life.

On the other hand, true happiness promotes serenity and inner peace. It draws strength from nobility of character and grows from within. In due course of time, irrespective of the fact whether a person is richly blessed by nature or not, lives in a village or in a city, is rich or poor, this happiness becomes a part of him. He begins to cherish it as the greatest gift from God.

The Path to Happiness

Perfect happiness cannot be attained through a magic formula received from one who has made it a part of his life. Everyone must attain it for himself. According to the Bhagavad Gita, happiness comes from peace of mind. This in turn comes from self-discipline. It is a plain, simple daily effort, which in course of time does not remain an effort. It becomes a habit. Happiness, then, will become as much a part of you as your limbs or organs.

Peace of mind comes from harmony between one's

thoughts and actions. Since no two persons are alike, their thoughts and actions cannot be similar either. However, people can have similar habits. Amongst those who have found eternal happiness, there are many habits that are conspicuously common. This makes the attainment of our goal as simple as incorporating as many of these useful habits in our everyday life as is possible through deliberate effort and practice.

Don't Live in the Past

It is rather strange to see that many people are unable to enjoy their present blessings because some of the unpleasantness of the past still lingers in their mind. It may be their unhappy childhood, lack of education, or an unfortunate incident, or something similar. Each time it comes to their mind it brings back the unhappy memories, as though it happened just today.

If you want to be happy today, do not give in to the unpleasant memories of yesterday. Why must you cling on to the past? It can only bring you morbidity and distress, along with the unhappiness that goes with such feelings. You must learn to enjoy what you have today, and not worry about what you could not have earlier. If you could not educate yourself earlier, you could do so now. If the memories of an unhappy childhood still linger in your mind, you could make up for it by helping a child in some useful way. You could offer repentance for past mistakes. Do not allow the unpleasantness to become a part of you.

Live for today and enjoy all the happiness you can find.

Keep Yourself Busy

Melancholic and unhappy thoughts always invade the idle mind. They bring along with them strange doubts and fears about ourselves and about those who are dear to us. In the beginning, many of our problems are only stray thoughts. However, through repetition in the idle moments of life, even the most imaginary problems become realistic, tormenting our peaceful existence. When we give in to these idle thoughts, we are really inviting quaint problems into our life. Since most of them have emerged from our imagination, there are rare chances of finding satisfactory solutions to get rid of them.

To be happy, learn to keep busy. Plan a balanced routine for yourself, allotting time for work, leisure, time with the family and for friends. But do not confuse rest or relaxation with idleness. They are not the same. In your daily routine, avoid monotony and fatigue. Develop new interests. Make friends. Spare time for some form of social work. When you are busy, there will be no occasion to think of imaginary problems. And you will be rewarded through a sense of achievement and happiness.

Positive Thinking

Most of us are buried under strange doubts and fears about our ability to make a mark in life. Our mind keeps prompting us negatively: "I cannot do it"; "I can't get it"; "I can't achieve it". Since the mind rules the body, it is not surprising that the body believes everything the mind suggests. We are left behind in life, causing us great unhappiness. While the world moves on in every sphere, we continue to live a life of stagnation – uneventful and dreary from beginning to end.

Now is the time to take a new look at the situation. It is not difficult to change our negative outlook towards life. It takes the same amount of effort to look at the brighter side of life as it does to look at the negative side. The results are certainly significant in making us successful. The magic lies in personal belief. When you believe that you are capable of doing something, your body believes it too. And releases the power required to turn the dream into reality. Positive thinking helps release this power, not once, but every time. This power may not promote you to become the chairman of your company right away, but it can surely add new dimensions to your personal ability. It can help you rise to the next higher position in the near future.

Make positive thinking a part of your daily life. Always look at the brighter side of things, even when it sometimes seems ridiculous. Positive thinking imparts a wonderful energy to you, not only aiding you in more efficient and successful living, but also in helping you radiate more goodwill and happiness around you.

Face Problems Boldly

Even the most affluent and blessed of people are not free from problems. Unfortunately, rather than accepting problems as a normal part of life, many of us see them as nature's conspiracy to pull us down. Many problems are but a creation of our own mind. Even when the problems are real, they are invariably not half as serious as we consider them.

Everybody has good and bad times. If it were not for the bad times, however, we would not work hard to make life a success. And we would take good times for granted. Everyone has his moments of joy, but there will also be occasions of grief, defeat and heartbreak. Both life and death are a part of human existence. Even the happiest of persons are not free from them. The only difference is that the happy man looks at the brighter side of problems and believes in his ability to find reasonable solutions. This is a shortcut for him through the period of trouble.

Whenever you find a problem is getting the better of you, write it down on a piece of paper. Note down the worst that could happen if you did not solve the problem. Then write down the steps you can take to avoid or mitigate the problem. When you have the details in black and white, you will notice that the sting has gone out of the problem and a solution comes almost of its own accord.

As you solve the smaller problems, you are then ready to solve the bigger ones.

Learn to be Successful

Nothing is more stimulating than success in our ventures. Most people feel that success comes only to a chosen few. Little do they realise that success is for everyone. It does not come from doing a few great things in life. Instead, it comes from doing the small everyday things of life in a great way.

Nobody can reach the top in a single attempt. One must rise one step at a time. To prepare yourself for the big successes that will eventually become a part of your life, learn to achieve success in small everyday activities at home and outside. They may appear rather trifling, but each small success achieved will prepare you for the bigger successes.

Don't be Selfish

Each one of us is selfish in some degree. From birth to death, we only think of our own needs. All our actions are motivated by personal benefit. Whatever we do, the shadow of selfishness is always with us. The more we think of ourselves, the more self-centred we become. This narrow outlook eventually makes us miserable and unhappy.

To overcome this problem, learn to share things. Selflessness increases feelings of self-worth and self-esteem.

Selfishness can be of two types. Firstly, in its common form, one seeks only personal benefit. Secondly, it is of the subtle kind where one's actions are beneficial to others also. We need to follow the latter kind. There is nothing difficult about it. Each day we do many little favours for our family, friends and the community. In return, though, we seek favours or expect them to be grateful to us. When favours are returned or gratitude acknowledged, however, our favours are neutralised.

Would it not be better if we did the little acts without a vested interest? We are then immediately rewarded in other ways. The goodwill sinks deep into our subconscious mind and projects through our personality, giving true happiness.

Build Good Friendships

The art of living happily is very much the art of getting along well with people. The better our understanding of human nature, the greater our happiness. In addition, who could be better than our own friends to teach us the great art of making and retaining friends? It is our relationship with them that we use as a guide in dealing with people in everyday life.

A good friend is indispensable. He stimulates us to greater heights of success. His companionship adds to our joy and takes the sting out of our sorrows. By pointing out our faults, a friend holds us back from excesses. In times of need, he helps willingly. By joining us in recreation, he helps in relieving tension.

To make friends readily, learn to be friendly. Do not let inhibitions hold you back from enlarging your circle of friends. Go out where you can meet people. Introduce yourself. A smile is the quickest way to dissolve barriers and invite immediate friendship. Encourage others to talk about themselves. A listener is always more welcome than the one who talks too much. In addition, when you listen to others, learn to accept views that may be contrary to your own.

In this wide world, different people will have different things to say about a common point. These differences can be useful, as they are very stimulating for mental growth. To enlarge your circle of friends, develop interest in a variety of subjects. But do remember that only those friendships last where there is harmony of thought and the relationship is reciprocal. Treat your friends as you would want them to treat you.

Count Your Blessings

Rather than enjoy what they have, many people talk about what they do not have. In today's competitive world, we will always see newer and better products marketed. Clever packaging and advertising stimulates our desire to possess them but few can afford to keep up with the stream of new products. Having to turn our face away from them creates a certain amount of unhappiness.

However, we need to understand that human needs are unlimited. But our resources to acquire these are limited. Therefore, we cannot allow our desires to go out of hand. Even if we had all the money to purchase all that we want, it would still not promote happiness. If this were possible, then the richest people would be the happiest of all. But this is not so. There are many with meagre financial resources who are still very happy. The secret of happiness lies elsewhere. The real needs of life are few and most people can provide these with some effort. It is the greed for the extras, which are not necessary, that gets us all wound up and unhappy.

If you want something, you will have to give something of equal value in return. So the next time you want something, think about what you can give in return. God has blessed you with a body that is capable of doing a lot. Besides this, each of us has many material benefits. Count your blessings and see which ones you can part with to acquire what you desire. You will soon realise how well off you really are and that you can do without having the new desire fulfilled. This will leave you feeling as happy as you initially were or perhaps happier.

Learn to Laugh

To be happy, one must learn to laugh. Laughter is the greatest of pleasures. It refreshes the tired, imparts good health to the sick and ensures happiness to everyone.

The person who can see the funny side even in the gravest of situations can never be defeated. Laughter eases and overcomes anxiety and tension. It immediately brings peace and happiness.

Learn to laugh naturally. Do not become too conscious about it. Share a good joke with your family and friends. Laughter brings people together. Coming from the heart, it gives strength. It creates as much peace within you as only a prayer can. It prepares everyone for truly happy living.

Slow Down the Pace

Some people are always in a hurry – at home, at work, or elsewhere. It is not that they are conscious of the utilisation of their time. Instead, they are impatient with everything.

To do one's work fast is fine, provided it is done efficiently. A man who is constantly in a hurry thinks he is efficient. In reality, it is otherwise. Impatience and haste promote fatigue and affect personal judgement, with the result that the person not only lives inefficiently, but also wears out his health soon.

Take it easy. Learn to be patient. Slow down the pace. Plan a reasonable routine. Make it flexible enough so as not to disturb you if there are unavoidable interruptions. Thereby, you will become more efficient outwardly, while inwardly you will experience more peace.

Be Moderate

Moderation is the greatest of virtues, but only a few of us realise it in time. We accept a particular way of life and then go to extremes with it. At one time, we are so happy that we overrate our good fortune. On another occasion, we lose all sense of balance and feel that nobody could be more miserable than we are. When one is moderate, failure and grief do not hurt too much, nor does success spoil one.

All the great seers and philosophers have commended moderation. Great men have practised it. Moreover, it can add new dimensions to your power for living a happy life. Do not give in to temptations easily. Initially, it may not appear too easy, but as you learn to weigh your decisions before you act, you will begin to tread the safer path of moderation. Do not go to extremes about considering every decision in such detail that you become indecisive. As moderation gradually becomes a part of you, it will bring tranquillity into your life.

Share Your Life with God

When we turn to God for inner peace, we turn to the great power that sustains the universe, our own world, and everything in it. It does not matter how we perceive this supreme power. God can help us cross the most difficult of hurdles and bridge the widest of gulfs.

You do not need to go looking for Him. He is right within you. Thank Him for all His blessings. Tell Him how grateful you are for everything. Ask Him to guide you. As you place your trust in Him, your needs will be provided.

Share your life with God everyday. Let Him guide all your actions. Communicate with Him. It does not matter whether you spend just a few minutes or more, but do this regularly. When you tell Him about your problems, He will provide the solutions and impart you peace and happiness.

The problem will gradually simplify and an answer will come. When you find it, do not forget to thank Him wholeheartedly.

Benefits of Meditation

When we share our life with God, we begin a partnership with a power that has no limits. We begin to like our conversations with Him. Not only are our problems solved, but we also begin to experience a new kind of peace within ourselves. Unknown to us, in accepting and talking to our partner, we are healing our inner self through meditation.

To meditate means to think fully and deeply – about our self. The word "meditation" is derived from the Latin root meaning, to heal. The more we meditate, the better we feel. Through meditation, we begin to understand the futility of our desires, of our greed and ignorance. As we avoid them, we heal our inner self. It is a profoundly personal experience. It guides us to a positive attitude in active life. It begins with good actions in day-to-day life. Gradually it takes us deeper into the inner self. In silence, we introspect about our thoughts and feelings, about what we experience in our life. In silence, one realises that we are a part of that great power that has been solving our problems.

If we are a part of it, we must have the attributes of that great power. We begin to feel and appreciate these attributes only through meditation. We feel the peace, the tolerance, love and goodwill. Life becomes a new and better experience. We do not look for happiness that comes from material acquisitions. It comes from within.

Many learn to meditate through the guidance and support of a teacher, a guru. If you are on the way to becoming the complete man, and have not found a guru, you need not be deprived from the happiness of meditation.

Choose a time that is convenient to you, preferably in the morning. Find a quiet corner, away from interruptions like the telephone. Sit comfortably on a mat or cushion on the floor, cross-legged, with your hands resting comfortably in the lap. If you find sitting on the floor difficult, you could sit on a chair with your legs resting on the floor, and hands on your lap. Keep the back straight. An upright spine helps the energy flow up and down. Take a few deep breaths.

Closing your eyes gently, think of God. He is formless. We know Him in many forms as Rama, Krishna, Christ, Mahavira, Allah or Buddha. Think of Him in whatever form you like. Repeat His name in reverence. Repeatedly surrender your ego to Him. Visualise His attributes in you – inner peace, tolerance, kindness and love. Thank Him for these qualities.

Day after day, as you repeatedly meditate, your craving for greater inner peace will grow. You will become a new person – peaceful, happy... the complete man.

Don't Give Up

Many of us take up a new thing in real earnest. It is not long before the novelty of the new idea wanes and we get back to our old way of life. Be especially careful when you accept the concept of eternal happiness in your everyday life.

The chances are that you have gone through this chapter rather hurriedly. Now that you know what it is all about, read it again, a little slower this time. As you read through the various points mentioned, and are reminded of certain areas of conflict in your own life, make a note of them. See what you can possibly do to overcome them. When you become conscious of their existence, you can make special efforts to eradicate them gradually. You can develop habits that are more useful.

Success comes from following your desire for happiness until you find it. Never give up.

Points to Ponder

- ❖ Happiness is our primary aim in life.
- ❖ Understand what happiness means to you.
- ❖ Lasting happiness comes from peace of mind.
- ❖ Yesterday is no more. Let it not spoil our happiness today.
- ❖ An idle mind is a storehouse of unhappiness.
- ❖ It takes the same effort to think positive as it does to think negative.
- ❖ Nobody is without problems. Look at the brighter side of life.

- ❖ Learn to be successful. Happiness will follow.
- ❖ Share your life with others.
- ❖ Make friends. They will add to your happiness.
- ❖ You are endowed with more blessings than you think.
- ❖ Laughter is synonymous with happiness.
- ❖ Slow down the pace. Live a moderate life.
- ❖ Share your life with God. Experience the joy of meditation. Never give up.

2. Developing Personal Magnetism

"Good nature is the very air of a good mind; the sign of a large and generous soul, and the peculiar soil in which virtue prospers."

-Goodman

Although the desire to look attractive is attributed more to women, men are as eager to impress others with their personality. It is this attractiveness or magnetism that makes it easier to single out the complete man even in a crowd.

To move ahead in life, a man must cast an image of himself that can give a fair idea of what he represents in life. First impressions may not always be right. However, a good first impression is an important factor that can make or mar the chances of favourable acceptance by fellowmen.

What Makes One Attractive?

We call a person attractive when he possesses a combination of qualities that delight us visually or mentally. An immediate thought is – what qualities delight the eyes and the mind most? Are these qualities a gift of nature, or can anyone develop them through personal effort? Are these qualities temporary or do they last a lifetime?

At birth, each person is blessed with a certain set of features. Attractive features alone are not enough. To be truly attractive, one needs to possess many other qualities. Nature has intended to make all things beautiful. It has endowed all of us with a great reservoir of power that we can draw upon to become more attractive. We only need to understand this great force and learn how to use it.

Becoming More Attractive

To look your best, first understand yourself. How do you rate yourself? Are you content with your looks, physique, health, education and environment? If you do not rate yourself highly, you cannot expect others to do so. Unless you believe in your ability to attract, you will not be attractive to anyone. To be attractive, one must learn to understand the ways of nature. Nature has made everyone and everything beautiful. If we are not satisfied with what nature has made us, it is our own fault. We must learn to take a positive look at ourselves.

To be attractive, good health is necessary. To be physically fit does not mean to have a special physique, but that you understand your limitations. If nature has made you weak in a particular area, do not feel dejected. Learn to live with these limitations. Nature has spared no pains to make our system perfect. However, when we burden our system with a heavier load than what the body can bear comfortably, stress affects the weaker areas, robbing us of our vitality. Therefore, learn to move at a pace that is in harmony with your health and ability.

To be healthy and attractive, the body will require its nutritive requirements. The needs are varied. However, all of them must be provided for. Milk, fruits and vegetables are rich sources of the vital substances that affect the skin, hair, eyes and the organs. They must form a good part of the daily diet.

A good posture and carriage, too, enhance personal attractiveness. As do good manners and a genial temperament. One is always attracted to a person who smiles effortlessly and speaks convincingly. A person who has his back hunched, stands leaning against walls and furniture, and walks uneasily cannot expect to look attractive. In the same way, the way you sit, walk, greet and meet people will decide how attractive you are to them.

The way you dress can draw immediate attention. Clothes speak loudly, but you must remember that elegance of dress does not necessarily come from expensive clothes. Clean, crisp clothes worn without much fuss always enhance personal charm. Everybody appreciates simplicity.

The face is the centre of attraction. It is also an index of one's thoughts. The main power of attraction comes from our thoughts. The more we can influence them, the better are our chances of success. Just as happiness and gaiety attract goodwill and well-being, feelings of anxiety, worry, anger and envy leave their telltale marks on the face. One must learn to be happy in order to radiate inner beauty.

A Healthy Body

A prerequisite for developing personal attractiveness is good health. The body is a complex structure that depends upon many functions before it can radiate good health and charm.

All the organs in the body depend upon the digestive system for nourishment. If the food we eat is varied enough to provide the nutrients required by the body, there is no need for concern. However, since our habits and tastes make us drift away from what nature desires, problems arise. We may be eating more than what we require, or perhaps not eating what the system really needs. The undigested food in the intestines releases toxins that make the functioning of the organs sluggish and rob the body of its buoyancy. Along with nutrients, it is important that the food provides sufficient roughage to keep the digestive tract functioning well. Fruits, vegetables and milk are necessary for every health-conscious person.

Since emotions have a marked effect upon the

digestive system, it is necessary that one learns to be calm during a meal and for a little while later until the food is digested.

Walking, swimming and various forms of physical work provide good exercise to keep a person trim. To be healthy, some form of exercise must be a part of the daily routine. This has the added advantage of increasing one's breathing capacity. The deeper one breathes, the more the oxygen available for the blood to absorb and pass on to the tissues in the body. No shallow breather can look rosy and healthy. Learn to breathe deeply. You could begin each day by sitting near the bedroom window and breathing deeply. Gradually your breathing capacity will increase to add on to your personal power.

The Skin

The skin wraps the body, helps maintain body temperature, provides a medium for excretion and, above all, reflects the condition of your inner health, making you look attractive. Skin condition changes with age. A baby is wrinkled because the skin is somewhat bigger for him. As he grows, the wrinkles fill out, making the skin smooth. Sebum, a fatty substance secreted by the cells on the skin surface, helps keep the skin moist, elastic and healthy. At puberty, the production of sebum may increase excessively, even clogging the skin pores. With advancing age, the production reduces and the skin becomes dry, less elastic, and begins to wrinkle.

The colour of the skin depends upon the quantity of a pigment called melanin. The sun tans the skin and can even cause sensitive skins to peel, but staying away from the sun soon restores its original colour. Since the skin is the index of inner health and the principal medium that makes a person attractive, it deserves good care and protection.

Body Care

It is easier to exercise rigid control on the external care of the body than on its internal care. The primary necessity is to keep it clean. One sweats more profusely in the hot summer months, but round the year dust settles on it and clogs the pores. This makes it necessary to keep it clean and healthy. For this, there is nothing better than a bath with plain soap and water.

A bath should aim at keeping the body clean. The process of soaping and then rinsing with cold or warm water is stimulating, as it promotes better circulation of blood. Massaging the body with oil before a bath also helps promote better circulation and keeps the skin soft and supple. However, vigorous massaging should be avoided. Massaging the body with oil may not be practical before each bath, but done occasionally it is useful.

For those who perspire profusely, particularly under the arms, an antiperspirant is useful. To ensure freedom from body odours typical in hot and humid weather, a deodorant is the right answer.

Personal Grooming

No man need be so vain as to powder his face as often as a lady. However, the way a man takes care to keep his hair combed, the teeth cleaned, the face shaved, the nails trimmed and maintains a general air of pleasantness reflects his personal sense of grooming. This is as important as the need for cleanliness.

A daily shave, a fortnightly manicure and a monthly haircut can make a man more attractive.

Poise and Manners

The way a person carries himself or deals with others in daily life reflects personal charm. The expression on your face speaks loudly about you. It is difficult to hide lack of confidence in oneself. Good manners too are as important as personal cleanliness or grooming. Manners reflect a person's background, his education and his ability to get along with other people.

In your daily living, cultivate all that you find good. Take particular care to build self-confidence so that it shows in your personal bearing and in your dealings with others.

The Voice

The way one speaks also reflects personal charm. Cultivate a pleasant and rhythmic voice. Speakers capable of holding the attention of listeners had not always been like that, but have developed their latent abilities through training and personal effort. To be a good conversationalist, take interest in the people around you. Make self-education a constant process. Stimulate your thinking through study, travelling and by meeting and learning about people. The more you know the better can you impress the people you talk to.

Speak well of people. If you cannot, it is better not to speak at all. Unpleasant facts are best not repeated.

The Wardrobe

Dress as well as you can afford to. Your clothes speak loudly about your tastes, disposition, likes and dislikes. Clothes draw immediate attention. Like personal charm, the clothes must delight the eye and the mind. The best rule is to dress for the occasion.

Clothes must be comfortable to wear, easy to care for, and elegant to look at. Expensive fabrics need not always be the most suitable for a particular need. Clothes must be such that permit maximum wearing. Take good care of them.

Clothes that fit well and are well cared for always attract a second glance. Do not wear the same clothes day after day.

The Power Within

External factors only help attract immediate attention. Beyond this, they cannot achieve much in promoting personal magnetism. To be attractive one needs to draw from resources deep within. Irrespective of one's external characteristics, each one is endowed with an inner power, which can be developed to work wonders.

Once we develop this, it becomes a part of us. We can effortlessly use it to influence everyone we come across. This power has distinguished all great men. To develop it for personal advantage one does not need to do great things, but to make the important little things a part of daily living.

Let us see how these important factors affect us and what we can do to make them a part of us.

Personal Magnetism

In school, one of the elementary lessons in physics is about the wonders of magnetism. It fascinated us to know how man had used this wonderful force to turn the wheels of industry. In geography, we learnt that the whole earth itself was a big magnet with its poles in the north and the south. The compass needle aligns itself with the two poles, irrespective of the place where it is placed. This enabled man to find his way around, even in the remotest corners of the world.

Each of us is like a magnet. We too have a magnetic field in which we exercise influence. Depending upon individual personality, the magnetic field may be small or large. This personal magnetism can be increased and with it, the areas of magnetic influence too. We can also lose our magnetic power, thereby reducing the magnetic field. This fact is of special interest to the complete man because he wants to increase his personal magnetism.

A magnet looks no different from a piece of iron of the same size and shape. The magnet's special power of magnetism comes from within, from the arrangement of molecules in a desired pattern. It is the same with human beings. It is immaterial what a person looks like externally. His magnetic power comes from within. External appearance does help in attracting immediate attention, but will fail to hold it unless it can draw from personal qualities that are not visible. Personal magnetism comes from such qualities.

Each one of us is a distinct personality. The sphere of our magnetic field is directly related to what extent we have been able to cultivate these power-giving qualities in our daily life. Our lives undergo continuous change, whether for the better or worse depends upon how we respond to our environments. We may not be able to change the characteristics inherited from our parents. However, if we can understand how the various environments affect us, we can appreciably adjust our responses so that we can ultimately benefit from them. The secret lies in the control of our mind.

The Mind – Our Master

The mind is our master. It is solely responsible for what we are today. On it depend our thoughts, feelings, attitudes and actions. It can raise us to the greatest heights of glory or drive us to a state of hopelessness.

The mind can send and receive messages through telepathy. It automatically attracts those with whom it is in harmony. This comes from the similarity of the frequency of vibrations in two persons. If the frequency is glaringly different, there is immediate repulsion. The frequency of these vibrations not only affects our relationships with people, but also our personal possessions.

Depending upon an individual personality, everything gradually comes into harmony within the mind. Success attracts success and failure attracts defeat and dejection. This makes the influence of the mind on our life apparent. If we can understand how it works, we can use it to advantage. At this stage, we need to differentiate between the conscious and the subconscious minds.

The Conscious Mind

It consists of the five senses of sight, smell, sound, taste and touch. These senses function when we are awake and put us into immediate contact with our environment. All our experiences are based on the messages received by these senses, which are then conveyed to the subconscious mind.

In the same way, the senses convey messages from the subconscious mind to the environment. The conscious mind is automatically switched off when we sleep.

The Subconscious Mind

To develop personal magnetism, the subconscious mind offers unlimited possibilities. The subconscious or creative mind becomes active as soon as a child is born and continues to function until death. It never rests and is responsible for keeping the body's vital functions in good state. It records all messages received from the conscious mind, processes them keeping in view past knowledge and experience, files them for future use or rejects them as harmful or unwanted. It is a great storehouse of knowledge, shaping our thoughts, actions, habits and attitudes. Since our well-being depends on these factors, the influence of the subconscious mind is considerable.

The initial experiences recorded in the subconscious mind come from the conscious mind's contact with the environment. We cannot exercise control over what has gone by, but we can still influence the subconscious mind through our thoughts, actions and habits that affect our attitudes. As we deliberately accept what is good and reject what is not, the subconscious mind releases creative power. This makes us physically and emotionally fit, promoting greater personal magnetism.

Building Blocks of Personal Magnetism

A habit is an act to which we are accustomed. Good or bad, the first time we perform an act, we feel somewhat uneasy. When we perform it repeatedly, the subconscious mind takes over from the conscious mind and we perform it almost effortlessly without even being aware of it.

Our life is the product of the cumulative effect of our habits, both good and bad. Our personality projects an image that is the result of the interaction between the good and bad habits. While every good habit adds to our personality, every bad habit detracts from it. Therefore, we need to develop more good habits and eliminate the bad ones.

To develop a new habit, we need to perform that particular act repeatedly although it may appear unpleasant initially. And to eliminate a bad habit, we need to avoid doing it although it may appear difficult. This is a matter of self-motivation. Visualise the harm the bad habit can do you. Consciously keep away from the circumstances that induce you to indulge in it. It will only be a matter of time and some effort before you will have added many good habits and eliminated bad ones. Then you will be well on your way to making personal magnetism work wonders for you.

Character

If we were to look for a single factor that promotes personal magnetism, the answer would be character. This is our most valuable possession. Its powers know no boundaries of colour, caste or creed. It easily overshadows the possession of riches, knowledge, intellect, or genius.

A man's character represents what he believes in. It can take him to the apex of glory and admiration, because it brings out all the virtues in him. But if neglected, it throws him into a slough of loneliness, failure and even ruin.

To develop personal power through character means to be dutiful, conscientious, truthful and honest. This is what all religions teach us. To convince you, these truths are written in many forms, illustrated through the lives of men and women who were perhaps no different from what we are. If you accept the principles of truthfulness, honesty and thoughtfulness and make them a part of you, you will have added a very vital force to yourself. This force has identified all great men who became immortal through their thoughts and actions. This force can extend the magnetic influence of a person over a very large area.

Character is made up of little day-to-day seemingly insignificant details of life. Every fleeting thought affects it. Thoughts become actions and actions turn into habits. The laws of action and reaction hold well with every little action we perform, although we may not understand it. All good and bad deeds are either rewarded or punished. Sometimes the results become apparent at an early stage. Even if they are not, points are scored in your favour, or against you, immediately.

The rewards of developing character in its noblest form are unlimited. As with all good things in life, before it can be achieved, there will be many hurdles and temptations. However, there is nothing that man cannot achieve through determination and effort. Thereafter, there will be a great power at your service. You will find the type of happiness you have never known before.

Controlling Thoughts

A thought is a precursor to every action. Our thoughts have made us what we are today. If you truly want to move forward, believe in your ability. You will reach the height you believe you are worthy of attaining.

There is magic in believing. What you believe, your mind conveys to every cell in the body. Thoughts of good health, success and happiness benefit every part of you, and those whom you come in contact with. Likewise, negative thoughts of sickness, failure, hatred, greed and revenge affect your life adversely.

You can transform yourself now. Visualise yourself as what you want to be. Believe in your ability to change. When the mind receives positive and constructive thoughts, one automatically develops personal power. If negative thoughts are entertained, there is a corresponding loss of power. The balance between the two decides what power one is capable of exerting.

This makes the need for positive thinking obvious. Unfortunately, 19 out of 20 people lean towards the negative. It takes the same effort to think positive as it does to think negative! The difference lies in personal attitude. Thoughts become actions and actions repeated turn into habits. These, in turn, affect our attitudes and thereafter the environment, completing the cycle. Our minds are conditioned by the environment and with such an overwhelming majority already in the grip of negative thoughts, habits and attitudes, the environment too gets charged with a high dose of negativity and the vicious circle goes on.

The environment feeds the mind with suggestions, both negative and positive. With greater negativism, the suggestions are more negative than positive and so is our receptivity. Try an experiment to study the influence of suggestions on a particular person. Have four or five persons meet him at intervals, at different times of the day. Each time let one person point out that he is looking run-down and perhaps needs to consult a doctor. By evening, the man will really want to visit the doctor!

The reverse is also true. A student scores well and takes greater interest in a subject when a teacher has suggested that he has a natural aptitude for the subject and he could do well in it. In the same way, an actor puts in a realistic effort because he is told that his acting is true to life. Such suggestions and thoughts play an important part in our lives.

Therefore, we should accept only those thoughts that

enhance our power positively and reject the negative. This may seem difficult. However, it can be achieved with a little effort. Just as in moments of absentmindedness one fails to register even a direct message, one can learn to deliberately close the mind to negative suggestions. This way one can learn to screen all thoughts coming into the mind.

To promote still greater power within us, we can practise what is popularly called autosuggestion. This needs some clarification. Each one of us is already practising autosuggestion. In most cases, we deliberately feed our minds with suggestions and thoughts that are not positive. Therefore, we fail to derive any benefit from them.

To make autosuggestion charge you with special powers, believe that you can become a more powerful person. You must believe that you are moving towards greater personal success and that you stand for all that is best in life – truth, honesty and thoughtfulness. As these strong beliefs seep into you, through repeated positive suggestions, note the wonderful effect they have upon you. See how these little thoughts transform themselves into constructive actions, which will become a part of you forever.

Controlling Emotions

Through the control of our thoughts, we also control our emotions. Emotions refer to our feelings of love, sympathy, kindness, fear, anger, hatred, envy and jealousy. These emotions can make or mar our prospects of success. Like thoughts, emotions are either positive or negative. They affect a person's health, professional success, family life and position in society.

Emotions need to be controlled not only for the great power that we can develop through positive ones, but also because of their distinct effect on our physical well-being and longevity. To keep feelings of disgust, revenge and hatred fresh in one's mind is to keep one's wounds green. One may succeed in making another person unpopular by giving vent to these emotions, but not without a significant detrimental effect upon personal power. Negative emotions rob energy and vital power, besides disturbing the balance of thinking and the physical functions of the body. The loss is still greater if these negative emotions continue to remain in the mind and through habit, become a part of the system.

Emotions like worry, envy, jealousy, hatred and fear are like invisible monsters, draining our system of vital energy. Worse, most of these emotions are not based on reality. We worry about calamities that never come and fear things that do not exist. We are envious, jealous and hateful without realising that we are only harming ourselves. The invisible monsters appear real only because we have allowed them to be anchored in our mind.

To convince you about the non-existence of these monsters, put down your worries and fears on paper. Note down what could be the worst that they could bring upon you. You will now have clear facts before you. Even if the worst is imminent, surely worry cannot avert it? Fretting and fuming can only reduce your power to face the problem. Once you have the problem sorted out on paper, go ahead and put the solution into action. Look at the brighter side and ignore the dark one. You will then achieve better results.

Emotions that can substantially add to your power are positive ones like love, kindness and compassion. Love yourself, your family, your work and the people around you. What you give of yourself to others is returned immediatcly. If somebody violates the faith you place in him, forgive him because forgiveness gives you strength. Hatred and revenge take it away. Only when the good effects of these positive emotions begin to accumulate will you be able to recognise the power they can add to you. You will then experience the growth of personal magnetism within yourself.

Developing Self-confidence

Lack of self-confidence holds back millions of otherwise capable persons. Some are held back by negative thoughts about their looks or physique, others by thoughts about their family background, and some by being unable to forget a none-too-pleasant past. To develop the magnetic power within, these insignificant thoughts must be overcome. With control of one's thoughts, feelings and actions, one is able to build new useful habits and a new self-confidence begins to grow. A man begins to find that he is no longer enslaved to sickly thoughts and feelings about himself.

A person must evaluate his personal capabilities from time to time. This gives him an opportunity to review his achievements and failures, and improve past performances. Keep revising outmoded thoughts of your personality. With effort, your power and capabilities will grow. Concentrate more on the activities in which you have achieved success earlier.

At the same time keep improving yourself through added knowledge and the power that is growing from within. Try your hand at new activities. Success is the best confidence builder. Keep repeating your successes. At no time should your faith in your personal ability suffer. Increase your interests. Read books on new subjects. Join a club. Learn to sing or play a musical instrument. Go out where you can meet new people and learn new things. With increasing confidence, your power will grow too.

The Power from Serving Others

Good and evil have existed on earth from the very beginning. Whenever man did what was good, he benefited from it in many ways. When he indulged in evil it might have brought him temporary pleasure, but in the end evil boomerangs and even destroys him.

A boxer keeps punching a bag with all his strength

because he knows that with each punch he is gaining an equal amount of power within his arm to prepare it for the bout on the great day. In the same way, as one ~~does a good act by helping someone needy, the feeling~~ of having reduced some discomfort or distress in the world proportionately increases one's personal power.

This is very clear in our vocations where better ~~service means more power in the form of money. The~~ social worker derives power not in the form of money, but through the increase of power in his personality. It is this fact that has motivated all successful men to devote at least some time to reduce some form of suffering somewhere, and for the rich to donate huge sums for good causes. As one gives a part of himself for the cause of others, it comes back manifold.

Smile at a person and you will get a smile in return. Be thoughtful about him and you will build goodwill. Help the needy, distressed and the suffering, and you will not only receive gratitude, but a powerful force within you. Keep multiplying your good actions and you will really be multiplying your personal power. Your influence will grow, firstly over a few, but gradually over a large area in your community and elsewhere. This new power will bring you happiness, good health and a long life when you shift attention from yourself to your family, the community and the country.

The Power from God

God is that powerful force that controls the whole universe. It is not possible to describe, comprehend and understand His powers fully. All religions agree that we can draw great personal strength from Him.

To win the goodwill of God, we need to understand the ways of nature. The closer we stay to nature, the more we can draw upon Him. Strength comes from developing an aesthetic sense for beautiful things handed down to us by nature. The beauty of the snow-clad peaks, the greenery of a thick forest, the shiny surface of a quiet lake, or the multi-coloured grandeur of a well laid out garden soothe us both physically and emotionally, giving us great strength. This is why people move away from cities to holiday resorts to be closer to nature. The more you can draw from it, the better it is.

A few moments spent every day in quiet communion with God are well spent. Talk to Him as you would to a friend. If you have God on your side, you have the most powerful force working with you and then there is nothing to fear. God will give you strength to cross the hurdles of life.

Using the New Power

With the development of a new magnetism within you, you will begin to develop a special instinct, an intuition or a sixth sense. This can guide you in giving a better vision of what is happening around you, or about what may happen. It is indeed a wonderful force and has set most people wondering about its many miracles. All men who have developed this power know that if used for the benefit of mankind, it grows. On the other hand, if used for evil purposes, this power wanes. It is a power that puts one in touch with nature's storehouse of knowledge. You can draw from it continuously for the benefit of mankind.

Points to Ponder

❖ Nature has intended all things to be beautiful.
❖ Beauty lies within every person.
❖ Good health is a prerequisite to becoming attractive.

- Poise and manners, the voice and clothes help one become attractive.
- Personal magnetism comes from within.
- The mind is one's master – for both good and bad.
- Habits make or mar one's personality.
- Character is the backbone of one's personality.
- Thoughts and emotions can be controlled.
- Self-confidence is the springboard to success.
- Power comes from serving God through His people.
- Well used, power grows. Misused, power wanes.

■ ■

3. Personal Health

"Health is the soul that animates all the enjoyments of life, which fade and are tasteless without it."

–Sir W. Temple

To be healthy means to have a sound body governed by a sound mind. A person is healthy when he is happy, enjoys his diet, eliminates waste products regularly, meets the physical responsibilities of life without undue irritation, and sleeps peacefully to prepare himself for yet another day. Subject to some variations, health is also considered in terms of weight, as linked with height, and with the absence of the feeling of fatigue. It is the sound mind that promotes cheerfulness, buoyancy and enthusiasm for living, typical of the healthy person.

The body is an intricate combination of several systems dependent upon each other for optimum functioning. Maintaining good health is a matter of keeping the functions in good order. Health is a personal matter and since the mind has an important influence upon physical health too, concepts of how healthy one feels vary from person to person.

Doctors consider a person fit when his body functions are within reasonable variations of the averages in the human race. Besides an external examination, doctors check the pulse rate (an average of 70 to 72 per minute), the body temperature (ranges from 97°F to 99°F, the average being 98.6°F), the rate of breathing (about 16 to 17 times per minute) and the blood pressure, which continues to change with age. Slight variations should not cause undue anxiety.

Develop Health Consciousness

Most of us shudder at the thought of suicide. Yet each day many of us are slowly killing ourselves through neglect of our needs. There can be no health unless one deliberately makes an effort to maintain it. If one were to move through life at a pace that the environment compels us to, the outcome would be none too happy. Nature has made each of us unique. What may be good for one may not be so for another. Each one must gauge his needs, understanding the areas of personal strengths and weaknesses. This is important because one may succeed in cheating others by pretending to be strong when one is not, but nobody can cheat nature.

People who live a healthy life are conscious of the need for good health. You too are the master of your own health. You have every right to be physically strong and healthy. Only you can exercise this right by developing health consciousness in everyday life. For this, prepare the mind for healthy living. Just as the mind can add to your personal magnetism, so can it give you continued good health. It is the attitude towards health that matters.

Soon after a man retires from active life in a business or profession, he begins to think that he is no longer capable of putting in his best efforts and perhaps his end is drawing close. What the mind believes, the body makes it come true.

Stress in Daily Life

If the environments could be such as to be in harmony with our habits and attitudes in life, there would not be much to bother us. However, the environment places certain demands on us. These, in turn, produce some stress within us, which could be of two types. First, that which affects our physical self and, second, that which affects our emotional well-being. These stresses make us tense and tired.

The stress affecting physical self is easily recognised

because we cannot carry more than what the muscles can support. The tension ensuing from such stress is relieved through rest and sleep. With time, one begins to realise personal limitations and tries to make fair adjustments in life to eliminate this form of stress.

However, the stress affecting our emotional well-being can be very different. It can build up without any physical exertion. If not kept within bounds, it can affect us at any time, can be habit-forming and cripple the strongest of people. The tension from such stress builds up very quickly. If not relieved through recreation, it manifests through physical ailments.

The stresses of daily living do not produce similar results in different people. Their effect depends upon personal attitudes towards various aspects of life. Each one has his weak spots. Initially, these act as safety valves for the tensions of living. An outlet in the form of an ailment slows the entire system, allowing it time to recuperate from the effects of stress and to make the necessary adjustments in personal attitudes to avoid further damage.

Coping with Stress

With competitive living, the need for coping with stress is becoming more important. We do not realise this early enough, as putting extra burden on the body is a gradual process. Initially, the body tries to adjust to the increased demands. In fact, this little extra burden helps prepare the body for emergencies.

However, if one continues to place a load on the system, it gives in when it cannot tolerate it any longer. One begins to suffer from minor ailments like aches and pains, fatigue, indigestion, headache, etc. However trifling these ailments may seem, particularly when one is young, these are signals to a person to take a new look at his physical and emotional health. Re-adjustments of habits to create a fair balance between work and recreation can restore normalcy. If one ignores the signals, there can be a serious setback.

In life, it is not possible to do away with tension altogether. However, we can learn to keep the level of emotional stress low and, through a suitable outlet find relief from it so that it may not cause any harm. For this, one needs to develop a positive attitude towards life and learn to always be happy. Analyse your daily life to understand and eliminate factors that promote tension. Is it your business or profession? The family? Finances? Whatever it is, find out how you can overcome it. You have a right to live the way you like. Adjust your attitudes to be in harmony with the environment. However, do not let anything enslave you. Prepare to face any situation.

Accept an important truth. We cannot change the people and the environment for these to be in total harmony with us. However, we can surely change our attitude towards them. We can learn to accept what is pleasant and ignore what is not. This should not be carried to extremes that affect life adversely. In this way, as we gradually learn to understand our needs, it becomes easier to avoid tense living.

Personal attitudes to finding pleasure in various activities differ from one person to another. Everyone needs to find out what suits him best. While some may find relief through outdoor activities like tennis, badminton and hiking, many prefer sedentary activities like reading, stamp collecting and music. Each is good to the extent it helps in relieving tension. (Read the chapter Forms of Recreation on page 157.)

Relief through Tonics and Drugs

To counteract the unpleasantness of common ailments that result from tense living, most people search for tonics and drugs to help them live a more competitive life free from such irritations. Many such tonics and drugs are available in the market. Thanks to their tall claims, many fall an easy prey to them.

Unless recommended by a doctor after a period of

sickness, such concoctions are unnecessary. These drugs only satisfy the psychological craving of having taken a tonic or drug to reduce fatigue. If not taken under proper medical supervision, many of these drugs can cause great harm. They can have sides effects, could be habit-forming and turn one into a drug addict, and may temporarily lessen the symptoms of a disease that requires early medical attention.

Prolonged use of these drugs may also produce immunity and they may fail to act when necessary.

Relief through Smoking

Most smokers cannot say why they smoke, but confess that they find it difficult to do without it. The fact that most people smoke more when under stress makes it obvious that they use smoking as a crutch to face common problems of life. While some people smoke to find relief from nervous tension, others do so simply because they enjoy it.

But researchers point out that smoking is a health hazard and affects different people in varied ways. It affects digestion, the lungs, the heart and the circulatory system. It can promote hypertension, heart disease and lung cancer. However, whether a person should smoke or not is a personal matter. Each individual is free to make the choice.

Once taken up, it is difficult to overcome. There is only one way to give up smoking – without a second thought. However, if one cannot, the best thing is to smoke in moderation. This way one saves both health and money.

Relief through Alcohol

Whereas the use of alcohol in small quantities improves appetite and promotes health generally, excessive use is harmful. Alcohol is one substance that is immediately absorbed in the stomach from where it passes into the bloodstream and thereon to the brain. Through depression of the higher nerve centres, it gives a false feeling of well-being. Alcohol also affects one's judgement of time and space, making driving after drinking very risky.

Social drinking is on the increase. The temporary pleasure of a feeling of well-being, accompanied with disregard for vexing problems, encourages people to drink in larger quantities more frequently. Like smoking, it is very much like a crutch for the problems of daily life. However, little do people realise that drinking in excess can irreparably ruin one's health. Alcohol does not offer a solution to the problems of life. It can only promote alcoholism and is best avoided. The long-term solution lies in adopting a suitable plan for living.

A Plan for Living

The secret of good health is to adopt and follow an intelligent plan for living. To ensure a lifetime of health, one must discipline the mind and body, and cultivate habits that promote good health.

The needs of the body are few and simple. It needs protection from the vagaries of the environment. It must be provided with the correct form of nutrition and some exercise. Waste products must be cleansed from the system regularly. These needs appear very simple. However, when we consider the many factors that affect the provision of these needs, we realise the need for good habits to make a plan for living successful.

To be effective, the plan must be in harmony with the basic nature of a person. There should be a fair balance between work and pleasure. As one makes the effort to live according to the plan, the result is the development of good habits to promote good health.

The primary need of the body is proper nutrition. One must regularly eat a balanced diet, rich in protein, with carbohydrates in proportion to the physical effort one puts in every day. Fats should be just enough to cook the food. Milk, fruits and vegetables must form an important part of it as they provide bulk, and add vitamins and minerals that are vital for good health. Eat food unhurriedly. Chew it thoroughly.

Emotions have a marked effect upon the digestive processes in the body. It is best to avoid work and worry at mealtimes. Do not overeat, particularly when upset. Also, do not skip meals. As far as possible, avoid eating at parties as you may eat an excess of the wrong kind of food. Eating snacks can also ruin an otherwise good appetite for a regular meal. Beverages like tea and coffee have a similar effect. Not all foods suit everyone. Many are allergic to certain foods. Avoid these. Finally, drink plenty of water.

Another vital requirement of the body is oxygen, which it takes from the air we breathe. Just as it is important to inhale fresh air, it is necessary that carbon dioxide be exhaled. The bigger our lung capacity and the deeper we breathe, the better the inhaling and the exhaling. Deep breathing near an open window the first thing in the morning can be very stimulating.

The importance of exercise cannot be overemphasised. It promotes both better breathing and circulation of blood. Exercise does not mean vigorous exercise. It should be gentle, the type one can continue with throughout life. Walking, swimming and cycling provide excellent exercise.

As the body uses the nutrition, various organs expel waste products to prevent contamination. Many of these can be very harmful if not cleansed from the blood regularly. The indigestible matter, along with some undigested matter, is passed out through bowel movements. The frequency of visiting the toilet is a matter of personal need and habit. A missed bowel movement should not cause anxiety. This could be because of insufficient roughage in the food. Correct this by including more fruits and vegetables in the diet.

The kidneys are responsible for the removal of most

harmful substances from the body by passing them dissolved in water as urine. The skin also performs a similar function, though only to a limited degree, by excreting some of the harmful substances as sweat. Anxiety affects this function. So does weather. One passes urine more frequently when frightened or worried, and during cold weather. Freedom from emotional blockades and drinking enough water keeps this function in good order.

Also important is the need for sufficient rest. Brief periods of rest during the day and sleeping well during the night help provide the normal requirements.

Obesity and Health

Many confuse obesity with good health. Proper nutrition is necessary for healthy living. If one eats the wrong kinds of food, or more than the normal requirement, it makes him obese. Being overweight makes a person liable to many health hazards. The extra weight places an additional burden on the organs that are supposed to handle only average weight. An overweight person could develop hypertension and heart disease.

A person is obese when he has excessive fat deposits in various parts of the body and is overweight. At no place in the body should there be fat an inch thick between the fingers. Compared to chest measurements, waist measurements must be at least three inches less, though five inches would be ideal. People do put on some weight with age. This seems to add to their personality. Under no circumstances should the increase be more than about 10 per cent of the weight at the age of 25 years.

Although obesity could be due to an imbalance of hormones, which cause excessive fluid retention, the basic cause is overeating. When a person eats more than what he requires, he lays it as fat in different parts of the body. Contrary to common belief, exercise does not help a person reduce. It helps in even distribution of weight all over the body. The real solution lies in cutting down on high-calorie foods, particularly fats and carbohydrates. Starvation diets are harmful. In any reducing diet, it is necessary to alleviate the mental craving for food. The diet must provide bulk in the form of fruits and vegetables that are rich in vitamins and minerals. Nutrition must be mainly in the form of protein, with sparing use of carbohydrates or fats.

Many health clinics offer special courses for slimming. They achieve this through exercises and control of diet, and sometimes through the use of drugs. There is positive loss of weight through these methods, but it is only temporary. A person will again gain weight unless he can become mentally conscious of the diet that is increasing his weight. The long-term solution lies in his mental approach.

The Defence System

We are attacked continuously by millions of germs as we breathe, eat and move about – and yet we stay fit! This is due to an inbuilt system of defence incorporated in our body by nature. There are many filters and antiseptics provided to counteract invasions day after day. Rarely do these germs reach the delicate interiors of the body. Even if some germs do succeed, there are white blood cells to take care of them. In case of a bigger attack, there are other cells to counteract the invasion and help maintain health. To deal with injuries, nature has provided that an injury should be washed with blood, and that the blood clot should seal the injury until the healing process is completed.

Even the organs are no less hardy. A person can

continue to live if the doctor were to remove the stomach, part of the damaged liver, part of the intestines, a kidney, or some other part. The body can still perform well when a lung is diseased or the heart is strained. The body's inbuilt system of defence gives the person every chance to live even under the most adverse conditions.

Science has further helped in increasing man's immunity against several diseases like tetanus, diphtheria, whooping cough, typhoid, cholera, plague, etc by producing antibodies. Considering all these factors, being in good health is as simple as maintaining the natural immunity of the body.

Normally, the inbuilt system of defence helps keep a man fit. But if he gives in to physical and emotional stress, his immunity could fall low, making him an easy target for sickness and disease. Therefore, remember to have proper rest during moments of increased stress.

Your Doctor

In all matters concerning health, the doctor is your best friend. Get yourself a thorough check-up at least once a year. If you have any complaints, do tell him about them. He may want you to consult a specialist. If so, take advantage of the specialised knowledge available today. Do not let any medical tests make you anxious, as these can throw light on many important factors. Medical science has made great progress and everyone is fortunate to have better medical aids available to ensure a healthier, longer life.

Living with Limitations

When a man is unable to understand the meaning of the body's stress signals in time, nature may place certain limitations to slow down his normal activities. These may be in the form of an ailment like heart disease, blood pressure, ulcer, diabetes, etc. Each of these will require medical aid, but should certainly not mean the end of an otherwise active and useful life.

Do not let fear harm you. You do not need to be afraid, but careful. Short spells of rest are now not enough. Change your outlook about life. Look at the positive side. Learn to be moderate with food. Under no circumstances should you allow your weight to increase unchecked. Keep your emotions within check. Do not smoke. Above all else, slow down your activities. Do not let stress overcome you.

You are the master of your own health. You can care for it and maintain it to enjoy old age, or let it slip beyond a decisive point.

Points to Ponder

❖ A sound body governed by a sound mind keeps one healthy.

❖ Good health begins with health consciousness.

❖ Stress is a part of everyday life. Learn to cope with it.

❖ Finding artificial relief from stress is like falling from the frying pan into the fire.

❖ Healthy people follow a plan for living.

❖ Understand your body's reactions.

❖ Your doctor can be your best friend.

❖ You are the master of your own health.

■■

4. Personal Problems

"It is not every calamity that is a curse, and early adversity is often a blessing. Surmounted difficulties not only teach, but hearten us to our future struggles."

–Sharp

Many men, well on their way to becoming the complete man, are faced with problems that they find difficult to discuss with others. The search for solutions is not easy. Here are subjects many men find difficult to discuss.

Boredom and Loneliness

Being in the grip of melancholic loneliness, many are bored with life. And there are others who are all on their own, but have no such complaints. Boredom and loneliness are a state of mind that may occur if we lack sufficient interest in the people and the surroundings in which we live. The narrower and more selfish our field of thinking, the more bored and lonely we tend to feel.

A long-term cure for this nagging problem lies in readjusting our thoughts and attitudes to appreciate what is good and to ignore what is not. However, any search for an ideal environment with ideal people living there would be futile. There is no Shangri-La. We can only dispel thoughts of boredom and loneliness by keeping the mind occupied with stimulating thoughts that generate enthusiasm for living. At the same time, we need to get over thinking about our problems and leave their care to nature, while attending to the needs of others. As we become selfless and self-sufficient, we find happiness and overcome boredom and loneliness.

Break the monotony of routine life through different forms of recreation. Be kind and sympathetic to others.

They may be waiting for this gesture from you, as they too may be lonely like you. Develop new interests and share these with others. With your interest growing in the larger interests of others and by shifting attention from yourself, you overcome boredom and loneliness, adding new dimensions in successful living.

Sexual Desire

The sexual desire in man is not totally instinctive. The environment in a civilised society is such that from the very beginning a rather suppressive attitude is taken towards the discussion of matters concerning this desire. Man becomes aware of this desire for the first time in adolescence. He finds that he is easily aroused, many times by trifling things. He feels rather self-conscious about this state, sometimes to the extent of doubting the normalcy of his feelings, and develops a guilt complex.

Society also makes a man conscious that it is his sexuality that makes his manhood significant. This point is stressed through cheap literature in which heroes are described as super-sexed individuals. Many men who unduly boast about their sexual prowess to impress their more gullible friends confirm this. It is not long before a normal man begins to worry about his own sexual desire.

Actually, most of these anxieties are ill-founded and must be banished from one's mind. The sexual desire in man is a natural desire and his emotions are such that he is easily aroused. This desire is at its peak from adolescence until about 20 years of age. Thereafter, it diminishes gradually until old age. The degree of sexual desire in individuals varies greatly, depending upon age, education, health, environment, marital status and one's emotional set-up.

Sexual desire does not arise from the genitals, but from an individual's mental attitude about it. The mind rules this important function. Contrary to what many men believe, not giving in to the desire does not promote health. It may only affect it adversely.

Personal Anatomy

Another fear that distresses many men is whether they are suitably blessed by nature to enjoy a healthy sexual relationship. There is no need for such a fear because there is no relationship between the size of the genital organ and one's ability to enjoy sex. Nor does this influence the partner's ability to enjoy a pleasurable relationship.

Size is an inherited factor and one reaches the full size during adolescence. There is certainly no correlation between one's physique and genital size. On an average, the male organ is about four inches long in the flaccid state and around six inches long when erect, though variations from four and a half to eight inches are quite normal.

Whatever be the size, a couple can enjoy sexual relations normally provided they make a mutual effort to understand each other's needs and aim for mutual fulfilment.

Sexual Fulfilment

Normally, a man finds sexual fulfilment through coitus with a woman. Society requires that for this to be legal, the union must be with one's wife only. Besides legal implications and religious recommendations, this carries some meaning. The purpose of coitus is not simply to find physical relief. It also provides emotional fulfilment when the partners unite with the common goal of making a home and raising a family. The institution of marriage is based upon these emotions.

Although many factors combine to make any marriage successful, the importance of a satisfying sexual relationship cannot be overlooked. Marriage makes the relationship an experience to look forward to.

Fulfilment in Special Circumstances

Even in normal married life, there are certain circumstances when a man may be in doubt about the ability of his wife to afford mutual sexual fulfilment. One occasion that arises each month, and lasts for a few days, is when the wife menstruates. Sex during this period is a matter of personal choice. Most couples prefer to avoid it. Since most women find relationships soon after the periods desirable, men wait ungrudgingly until then, as coitus can be especially pleasurable with this heightened desire.

A few women do not mind having sex even during their menses. The choice rests with the couple. If they do not find it unaesthetic, and can enjoy it, there is no harm.

Another doubtful occasion is when the wife is pregnant, or soon after confinement. A couple can continue to have sex until about six to eight weeks before the baby is due. As the pregnancy progresses, it is advisable that the husband exerts less pressure. In the later months, it is also advisable to use only those positions that do not put undue pressure on the wife's belly.

Other Forms of Sexual Relief

Since lack of fulfilment of sexual desire can adversely affect a man's mental set-up, some men turn to deviations for sexual relief. This may only be a temporary phase. In a few rare cases when a man is emotionally unstable, it may be on a regular basis. Sex being rather personal, such deviations often leave a guilt complex, causing great anxiety and distress. Once again, these fears are ill-founded and occasional indulgence in such deviations does not affect a man's normal sex life.

At some time or the other, almost all men indulge in masturbation or autoerotism. There was a time when all the ills of mankind were attributed to masturbation. It is now an accepted fact that this is not harmful per se, nor does it affect normal sexual life. It is widely practised by the youth who do not have partners for normal relief, as well as by some adult men occasionally. It does give physical relief, but is totally devoid of the emotions involved in a normal relationship between couples. Therefore, one cannot find complete fulfilment in this way.

In the absence of a partner, to find sexual relief some men may indulge in homosexuality temporarily, especially in prisons, camps, etc. When a man prefers this to normal sexual union, it is referred to as homosexuality. In many cases, this practice may leave behind a sense of guilt.

Sexual union with a prostitute or a willing female partner may offer greater physical pleasure than other forms of relief. In reality, this can be likened to masturbation, as it does not offer any emotional fulfilment.

Does Sexual Relief Weaken?

When a youth is compelled by his impulses to be more indulgent in seeking sexual relief, he is often worried if this could make him "weak". As the man reaches the pitch of excitement, culminating in ejaculation, an intense pleasure vibrates through every part of his body, the tension ebbs away and soothing sleep overtakes him.

This soothing fatigue, accompanied by the loss of millions of generative cells suspended in a nutritious medium, seems an unnecessary, though pleasant, waste of body nutrition. The childhood feeling that anything pleasant is necessarily bad furthcr creates fear.

However, there is nothing to fear. The relief of normal sexual desire promotes physical and emotional health. The body continues to produce semen at a specific rate and until the time it is used, this is stored. The quantity of discharge decreases if one indulges more often than what the body can cope with.

Similarly, if indulged less frequently, the quantity is more. Regular sexual relief keeps the reproductive organs in good condition and a person continues to enjoy good health.

Sexual Stimulants

Men have always been looking for food and drugs that could increase their sexual desire and the pleasure derived thereof. They have tried everything ranging from pornography to surgery. Many believe they have been successful.

However, the truth is that nobody really needs these aids. If a man is able to enjoy sex more at one time than at another, the secret may really lie in his mental approach towards the relationship. Although most users affirm that alcohol, marijuana, LSD and some other drugs increase desire and pleasure, the fact is these drugs do not increase sexual pleasure. The increase in pleasure is due to the lack of inhibitions after the use of these aids.

Many people believe that nourishing foods also increase sexual desire, but there is no truth in this either. The reason why people find some foods stimulate them sexually is because they mentally attach great importance to these foods and each time they use them, they anticipate more pleasure from the union.

The only thing that genuinely increases sexual desire in man is the use of the male hormone testosterone. However, its use is not advisable until there is clear evidence of its deficiency in the body, characterised by the lack of male characteristics. If testosterone is injected into an otherwise normal person, it could later have adverse effects.

The best stimulant is a healthy attitude towards sex, free from fears and inhibitions. The secret of a satisfying relationship is in winning over the co-operation of one's partner and enjoying mutual pleasure.

SECTION–II

Impotence

Another distressing problem is the fear of impotence or the inability to perform. This may or may not be accompanied by the lack of sexual desire. In coitus, the role of a woman is comparatively easy. She may not desire or enjoy sex, but she is still fully capable of performing by receiving the male organ.

But the man's role can be rather demanding. Before he can perform, he must achieve an erection, which must be lasting in order to make an entry, and then control himself from reaching climax until the couple can find it mutually satisfying. If a man fails to achieve or sustain the erection, the condition is referred to as impotence.

In this, a man may not achieve an erection at all, or his erection may fail before he can penetrate. The reassuring news is that all men experience some form of impotence at some time or the other. In most cases, the underlying cause is anxiety, worry and emotional stress. Physical causes are rare compared to psychological causes. A man needs to understand that these negative emotions can always affect him adversely. One should not give in to them.

In most cases, if the man can speak frankly to his partner, many of the fears simply vanish. An understanding wife who reassures and encourages her husband is always a big asset in setting things right. In rare cases, it may be necessary to visit a doctor. This should not arouse anxiety, as the condition can be treated.

Infertility

When a couple are unable to beget children, it may be that both the husband and wife have a low level of fertility. In many cases, only one of them could have a problem. If the husband has a problem, it could be due to the inadequacy of seminal discharge. It is also possible that there are no sperms (male cells which fertilise the ovum in the woman). Or they may be insufficient in quantity or have low vitality and are unable to reach and fertilise the ovum. The absence or lack of sperms can be due to poor production. It is also possible that the ducts through which the sperms move are blocked.

Besides these, there can be other reasons for this problem. It is necessary to consult a sex specialist who can positively help in identifying and curing the problem.

Birth Control

Never before has there been freer discussion recommending various methods of birth control. Yet, many people are hesitant about solving this crucial problem. It is a problem that the husband and wife should resolve mutually.

All methods of contraception have the same purpose: to prevent the sperms from fertilising the ovum during sex. The ovum is released about 14 days before the onset of the next menstrual flow. Allowing three days before and after this day for variations, the lifespan of the sperms to be completed, and the ovum to pass out unfertilised, it would be safe to have sex at any time other than this crucial one-week period. This method of contraception, known as the Rhythm Method, is the most natural way. Since this method does not offer adequate protection, and entails total abstention during the crucial one-week period, it is not very popular.

Besides, there are many other methods that can be used by the woman. A cap fitted to cover the entrance of the uterus (to be initially placed by a doctor), foaming tablets, capsules or gels squeezed up high in the vagina with an applicator, all offer varying degrees of protection, but find limited acceptance. Many couples find these inconvenient, as they have to be used each time before sex, interrupting the spontaneity and some are also somewhat messy for the woman. The IUCD (intra-uterine contraceptive device), or loop as it is popularly called, offers good protection, though it may not suit all women.

However, the method that offers the best protection and allows sex to be spontaneous is the Pill, which the woman needs to take orally for 21 days of the menstrual cycle. It has found global acceptance, particularly among educated women.

The most elementary method of contraception used by men is abstinence, as in the Rhythm Method. Another method, coitus interruptus, entails withdrawing the male organ at the time of ejaculation so that the seminal fluid is not deposited inside. This is not a satisfactory method.

The most effective method for men is use of the condom, a thin rubber sheath worn over the male organ. This acts as a physical barrier and, during ejaculation, the seminal fluid collects in a pouch at the tip of the condom.

A permanent contraceptive measure is vasectomy, which renders a man sterile through a simple operation performed under local anaesthesia that closes the passage through which the sperms pass. This does not otherwise affect normal sexual activity in the man.

The choice of a suitable method of contraception ultimately rests with the couple. Preferences will vary, but with some experimentation it should not be long before a couple find what is acceptable to them.

The Change of Life

Sexual desire in man is at its peak from adolescence until he is about 20 years old. Although he will be capable of reproduction until he is 70 years old or in some cases even later, with advancing age his sexual capabilities decrease. A significant change may occur during the 40s or later. In many ways, this can be compared with the menopause in women when their reproductive life ends. In man, the change is more gradual. Unless the man understands the cause, it can be a frustrating experience for him.

At an advanced age, his inability to enjoy normal sex bothers the man. He may fail to achieve normal erection, thereby rendering him impotent. On the other hand, after menopause with no fear of an unwanted pregnancy, the wife's interest in sex may increase, which the man cannot fulfil, and it may disturb him emotionally, affecting his health.

This inability to perform results from a reduced production of the sex hormone testosterone in the body. Besides sexual ability, it also affects male characteristics. The beard may begin to thin down, the breasts may enlarge, the penis and testicles may begin to shrink and the man may not remain as upright as he used to. Depression, anxiety and irritability will also accompany this. All this is normal, but worrying about the condition only makes it worse.

The best solution lies in visiting your doctor, who may recommend a preparation containing testosterone. This can reverse the symptoms and bring sexual activity back to normal. An understanding wife can be a great asset in reassuring the husband.

There is no reason why the couple cannot continue to enjoy sex until the last days of their lives. An understanding couple need never consider themselves too old for the pleasures of lovemaking.

Points to Ponder

- ❖ There is no place for boredom and loneliness in the life of a complete man.
- ❖ Understand your body and your sexual desire.
- ❖ A controlled sexual desire is a great force in life.
- ❖ Problems are a part of normal life. Understand them.
- ❖ There is a solution to every problem. Find it.

■ ■

THE FAMILY MAN

Nobody is complete by himself. Neither are you. If it were so, the institution of marriage would have died long ago. If this institution is under great strain today, it is not because it stands upon a hollow foundation. Marriage has withstood the test of time. However, it is an individual's attitude towards marriage that is to blame. With several factors affecting the relationship, degeneration sets in unwittingly. We look forward to marriage as a one-way street, which it is not. Take a positive attitude towards the relationship. It adds on to make a person complete.

A competitive atmosphere at work has compelled individuals to pay greater attention to their vocations than to their families. Young children have been affected the most. Present-day children are better provided for than ever before. Yet, in terms of quality love and care, they never suffered as much. The younger generation is smart, well dressed and educated. But never before were as many young people carrying invisible scars in their minds – all the result of parents who provided well, but failed to give quality time and quality care to them.

You cannot be complete without your family. Their happiness is as important as yours. Learn to be a good husband and a good father. It is not difficult. You can make your marriage a great success. Your wife can contribute substantially in making you a better person, a complete man. Your children need you. Give them the love and care that is their right.

In due course, they will repay you in equal measure. It is just a matter of setting your priorities right.

1. Love and Marriage

"First get an absolute conquest over thyself, and then thou wilt easily govern thy wife."

–Fuller

Your wife is the most important woman in your life. The day you accepted her 'for better or for worse', a new life began for you, just as it did for her. A wife means a lot to any man. He looks forward to her providing him companionship, a happy home, and becoming the mother of his children. These are not temporary needs. They must be met each day throughout life.

Marriage binds a man and a woman for lifetime. While it provides them an ideal medium through which they can mutually fulfil their needs, it also throws up certain problems, which are obvious when two individuals come intimately close and stay that way throughout their lifetime.

Although the give-and-take attitude is the basis for a couple uniting in holy matrimony, individuals being what they are, they not too infrequently overlook the partner's needs, giving rise to conflicts. It is important for every couple to mutually make the best of their marriage.

Therefore, it is necessary that marital conflicts be avoided as far as possible. If conflicts arise, they must be suitably resolved. Each partner must understand the needs of the other, thereby helping the other find fulfilment.

Marriage Today

The institution of marriage is undergoing continual change. There was a time when man took on the role of an unquestioned master and guide. The woman followed him, taking his word to be law. Marriage is a lifelong partnership between a man and a woman, based on feelings of love, companionship and mutual welfare.

The present times permit a freer selection of a partner. While the parents may still insist on satisfying themselves about any proposed match, there is every opportunity for a couple to meet each other before an alliance is finalised. This affords each a chance to know the other better, but there are still several problems that continue to make marriage a big gamble.

The number of divorces are rising, bringing not only heartache to the couple, but also endangering the future of the children from such marriages. While some feel that it is better to break a marriage than to live a life of discord, in most cases wrecked marriages have resulted from lack of tact and understanding, from intolerance and selfishness.

What is Love?

To be forever satisfying, love can be defined as the emotion that encourages intelligent self-expression in the partner and creates a congenial atmosphere where the couple can find more happiness together than individually. This emotion grows gradually in intensity. It is based upon patience and mutual understanding. One must learn to express this kind of love. What one gives comes back manifold. Any marriage built with a clear understanding of this concept of love can stand the greatest of stresses, and ensure a life of harmony and happiness.

Understanding the Wife's Needs

The first few weeks, or even months, of a marriage can be rather deceptive. They come and pass like a dream, leaving behind only sweet memories that can set anyone's heart racing. This is a period when the couple whisper promises into each other's ears – promises to be faithful, to build a happy home and to give a new meaning to life.

Unfortunately, many of these promises are short-lived and the realities of life suddenly arouse the couple from their pleasant slumber.

For the first time the man begins to realise that marriage is more than just pleasant companionship with a woman. There is need to understand what she is and not what he thought her to be. It confuses him that she contradicts herself in many ways. At one time, she is a pillar of strength; at another time she snuggles into her husband's arms, making it obvious that she is helpless and needs security. Generosity and benevolence give her strength, but on another occasion, she may act miserly. She can be kind and yet very harsh and hard-hearted. Tears come as easily to her as does laughter. All this and much more... However, not without feelings of utter amazement, frustration and helplessness in the husband.

The all-important questions now begin to dawn in the husband's mind. What do love and marriage mean to his wife? What does she expect from him? How can he ensure harmony in their marriage?

A woman expects her husband to provide companionship and security through a reasonable home, a steady living, and a respectable place in society. Besides this, she looks forward to his becoming the father of her children. While these needs appear simple enough to provide, they must be fulfilled day after day throughout life. Furthermore, since the wife will have her own ideas about how these needs should be fulfilled, many problems can arise.

In trying to understand the wife's needs better, a man will do well to know that the emotional set-up of a woman is very different from that of a man. A woman may be physically weaker than man, but is endowed with greater inner strength and perseverance. She can be very sentimental about love. When she believes that a man loves her, she looks forward to his affection not through sporadic expressions, but in the form of little day-to-day gestures. While to a man the expression of love comes suddenly and flows out as rapidly, a woman looks forward to it in small doses all the time.

Understanding the wife's needs is a continuous process. One learns a little each day through hit-and-miss methods. Be frank and straightforward. Ask her about her personal hopes and aspirations. You can learn a lot by observing her reactions in daily life. The moment you understand her basic needs, and then make a positive effort to help her realise her desires, you will be well on your way to achieve harmony in your relations with her.

Helping Her Help You

If you want your wife to help you, you should first be willing to satisfy her personal needs. As a wife, she might have accepted you as her unquestioned leader and guide, but as an individual, she has her ambitions, hopes and aspirations that need to be translated into reality. She expects her relationship with you to promote her cause and to increase her self-confidence. She expects you to respect her feelings and to have faith in her ability. She feels that this is a fair means of finding mutual satisfaction in marriage.

Through little acts of thoughtfulness, convince her that you care. Give her the respect that she rightly deserves. Make her feel that your marriage has enriched both of you. Take particular interest in her looks. Every woman hopes her husband will find her attractive. Compliment her as often as you can, but do it sincerely. While ensuring that your wife enjoys a pleasant self-image, also make certain that you look well yourself. Dress appropriately. She wants to feel proud of her relationship with you and the better the image you project of yourself in society, the happier will she be.

To a woman, her home and family are a medium

through which she can express herself. She attends to the home, cares for the children and her husband and does the best she can to project the image of a happy contented family. Her life revolves around these activities and even if you fulfil the entire financial liabilities of maintaining the home, you must appreciate her efforts in managing the domestic affairs well. At times, she may not be able to present a particularly palatable meal or clean the house. Such things should be accepted as part of normal life. Criticism, as far as possible, must be avoided; but if you must, then ensure that it is only constructive criticism that you make.

Do not make the children her individual responsibility. She will keep them clean and well fed just as you pay for their upkeep. A father who is indifferent to their needs for paternal companionship and guidance can be irritating to both the wife and children. Their upbringing should be a joint responsibility.

The wife will want a certain amount of money to run the house. Help her draw up a budget for the household expenses. Do not encourage her to spend more than what is allocated under a particular head. Do not ignore her personal monetary needs. She must have a fixed sum that she can use as she pleases without having to account for it.

What may appear to be a comfortable and pleasant duty of running the home may not really be so. Repetitive work produces monotony, boredom and fatigue. If the husband does not make an effort to offer her a pleasant change from ordinary life, she does have reason to be irritable and disagreeable. Therefore, arrange your time and working schedule to allow you both occasions to take a stroll, meet friends or perhaps go for a movie.

Togetherness can be stimulating, but too much of it can be very irritating. So, do respect her need for privacy. Do not insist that she should tell you everything. Let it come voluntarily. In the same way, let her enjoy personal interests and hobbies. Encourage her to do better. Give her every opportunity for self-expression and creativity.

Women can be sentimental about their birthdays and wedding anniversaries. You will do well not only to remember these two important dates, but also to surprise her with a little gift each time. You could help her with some household chores occasionally, or even baby-sit while she takes some time off with her friends. The little breaks help release tension in her daily life and not only promote efficiency, but also enable her to offer undiluted companionship to you.

The Physical Side

Books of all hues on the subject of sex and marriage are freely available in the market. Yet, many hesitate to buy and read books on sex for fear of what others would think. They still associate sex with something shameful and dirty. On the other hand, many feel that they know all that is there to know about it.

Books about sex and marriage can teach a lot about the basic nature of man and woman. They are often illustrated with case histories and speak about general trends. However, these books present one problem. Many readers accept certain standards described in the books as ideal. If they cannot meet these standards, they begin to think that either they or their partners are abnormal. Little do they realise that individual needs vary significantly and their anxiety about the relationship is harmful.

The art of lovemaking cannot be mastered overnight. For any couple, it may take anywhere from a few months to a few years to do so. Many learn it long after they are blessed with children. Others never master it at all.

Love means different things to the husband and to the wife. To learn the art of lovemaking, it is necessary to understand this difference. A man is easily aroused.

To him love and sex are the same thing. His emotions are active, forceful, rise swiftly and wane as rapidly. On the other hand, a woman is slow to arouse. To her sex means love. She likes to be loved and caressed. Her emotions are passive, receptive and rise gently. This makes her feelings a constant challenge to the husband. She must be won over every time before they reach a common level of desire for each other.

Other factors can also arouse anxiety. There may be variations in the size of the sex organs. Due to health reasons, the sexual urge can be at low ebb. However, such factors should not worry the couple because if they are mentally compatible, they can surely overcome such problems.

Expectations from the wife in such matters present the real problem. While a man expects his wife to be a perfect angel when she moves about with him in society, he expects her to be a perfect mistress when she is in bed. He expects her to be as receptive to his advances as he is forceful, but despite the efforts, she is rarely as responsive as he would like her to be.

This sets the man wondering whether he is being unreasonable in his demands. Or is the wife to blame? The fact is that both are right in their respective positions. Their nature makes them so. While the man's passions may be aroused even by trivial thoughts, a woman's emotions do not make her as responsive to his advances. To be aroused for sex she needs to be wooed each time. For her, the enjoyment of sex comes only after the pleasure of being wooed. The initial love-play prepares her mentally and physically. Therefore, do not demand sex as a right, but only as an act of mutual pleasure and satisfaction.

To make marriage physically satisfying, get to know each other. Give up inhibitions, if any. Discover each other. Learn to fondle and caress her. She is responsive to certain erogenous zones in her body around her eyes,

74

ears, nose, lips, tongue, nape of the neck, armpits, breasts, buttocks, thighs and the genital area. Of course, not all women respond in the same way to a particular erogenous zone, but it should not be long before a husband finds out what gives his wife most pleasure. During the process of love-play, be patient and gentle.

Initially, when a man learns to arouse his wife for mutual sexual satisfaction, he has problems controlling his feelings. This can be difficult and trying. If the couple display understanding, patience and some restraint on the husband's part, it can help bring about a fair adjustment suitable to both.

Another problem that all men face at some time or the other is when the wife is unresponsive despite ardent wooing. This can be due to several reasons. Women are more responsive to lovemaking on certain days of the month. Health, fatigue, emotional upsets and the environment affect their responsiveness. Fear of an unwanted pregnancy can also play a role. An uncomfortable posture, a misplaced uterus, or some infection that makes sex painful, can affect a woman's responsiveness. But if the couple can discuss each other's problems and resolve to solve them, there is no reason why sex cannot be mutually satisfying.

An Ideal Pattern

From what has been discussed about the physical relationship in marriage, can we deduce an ideal pattern to make marital relations more mutually satisfying?

The fact is that no hard-and-fast rules are possible here. Depending upon age, health and living conditions, some couples have sex daily. Others may have it once a month or more infrequently. The average for a middle-aged couple is twice or thrice a week.

Sex is a personal affair. What is enjoyable or detestable to one may not be so for the other. Do not use language that your wife may consider crude or vulgar. Neither should you discuss your sex life with friends, however close they may be. A woman likes to be secretive about her sexual likes and dislikes. If you do not honour these sentiments, it may land you in trouble.

Sex must not be a rigid ritual followed in detail from time to time. Men find variety stimulating, but women are slow to change. Some are even averse to it in some ways. Be patient and tolerant. Experiment tactfully. Search for new joys. Find out what is mutually most pleasurable. Let each session be a spontaneous act preceded by love-play. Enjoy satisfying your partner until both of you not only long for physical pleasure, but find it a sublime emotional pleasure too.

Attitude towards Money

Money is the root cause of several problems for many couples. While many wives feel their husbands do not give them enough to run the home, most men complain that their wives are spendthrifts. In their own way, each of them could be right. For domestic harmony, it is essential to have a fair understanding between the husband and wife about their personal finances. This becomes all the more important when we find that wives can be equally efficient bread-earners.

In such cases, should the couple pool their income and meet the expenses jointly, or should the wife retain her income, with the husband paying for household expenses? Most couples have varied views on such matters.

Most men have faith in their wives and each month unhesitatingly hand over their salary, or a fixed amount, for household expenses. However, some men avoid giving them enough money, not realising the stress the wife then undergoes. While some women may be spendthrifts and give little thought to the limitations of the husband's resources, the solution does not lie in withholding money. It is preferable to explain the situation to her. In some cases, a husband can be equally guilty of wasting money. Sometimes husbands spend excessively on the pretext that since they earn the money, they have every right to spend it for their personal pleasure. Either way this can ruin an otherwise happy marriage.

In most cases, financial tussles arise from a lack of proper communication and understanding. Expectations on either side can be high and this can influence personal judgement. To achieve harmony in personal finances, be fair and frank with your wife. Tell her what you earn and what you can give her every month for household expenses. Do give her some money for personal needs. To convince her about your fairness in financial matters, tell her exactly what you spend on yourself.

If she so desires, you can help her draw a budget for household expenses. If she too is working, then reach a fair settlement about individual responsibilities for meeting various expenses and saving some money for future use. Above all, remember that there is no place for suspicion if you want harmony in your married life.

Other Problems

Few marriages, if any, are free from problems. If these are not checked in time, they can assume dangerous proportions, affecting family life as a whole.

The man's attitude towards marriage can create serious problems. Surprisingly, many men consider their domination and aggressiveness towards the wife as normal behaviour. This attitude might have been all right decades ago. Then women spent all their time at home. Today, when women have shown their ability in a wide variety of fields, even becoming equal breadwinners, there is no place for such concepts. Marriage is now an equal partnership.

If you don't want your wife to desert you, be tactful and understanding, accepting her as an equal, and be gentle rather than domineering and aggressive.

Strangely, there are some relationships where the wife may be bossy. She may come from a richer family, may be more educated, or perhaps she may be more capable with the use of her tongue. She will insist that she understands the world better and therefore must wield power in the interests of the family. This can give the husband a serious complex that may not only be an embarrassment in daily life, but also result in great loss of confidence in his own abilities. Gradually, he may seek her advice even on trivial matters.

Although the wife's attitude may be skewed in this instance, the husband is equally to blame for giving in. Many henpecked husbands claim that they act diplomatically to buy peace at home. However, this can harm both and affect their standing in society. Firstly, this problem should not be allowed to take root. However, if it already exists, do not waste another day in tackling it. Get down for a heart-to-heart discussion. It may be difficult, but you have to do it. Discuss mutual needs and how to fulfil them. Formulate a code of behaviour in the home and outside. Develop the new habit gradually as you shed the old complexes.

Another problem, particularly if the wife is attractive, is jealousy. Most men deny it, but generally men tend to be more jealous than women are. This may arise from the husband's lack of confidence in himself. He may feel that he is not capable of keeping his wife interested in him. If he has to keep away from home for long stretches of time, he may not be able to satisfy her sexual needs. However, the feeling of jealousy is mostly ill-founded. There is no place for this in marriage. It can ruin an otherwise happy marriage.

The solution lies in building one's faith in his personal ability to keep the wife pleased and happy. Encourage friendships with couples rather than with bachelors so that there are lesser chances of suspicion and jealousy. You will do well to remember that women do not love their husbands for their looks. It is feelings of love, kindness and understanding that bind a couple together.

Finally, there is the common problem of a nagging wife. Nagging literally means finding faults over trivial things. Most people consider this as a woman's weapon against man. The tongue can sting sharper than a whip. Nagging can assume irritable levels in some marriages. However, the husband needs to understand that most of the time nagging is no more than a relief from tension for the wife who has a monotonous routine of household work. In most cases, she has no malicious intent and is just getting a complaint off her mind.

Few husbands can help the wife get over this habit unless she is eager to do so herself. Therefore, the best solution is to receive it with pretended concern. Men who have learnt this trick hear the complaints with professed sincerity, showing concern, but smile inwardly as they have their mental receiving station switched off!

Husband-Wife Quarrels

Basically, a man and woman enter married life with the selfish motive of furthering their personal needs and fulfil the partner's needs as a price for the same. Most partners know that they cannot get what they want unless they give an equal amount in return.

Nevertheless, with one's personal needs uppermost in mind, not too infrequently one loses the balance, giving rise to protests and perhaps a quarrel. Many times the expectations from a partner can be unreasonably high, and with desires out of proportion to the real needs, discord sets in. While some minor quarrels can help in keeping the marriage as a happy relationship, it is best if quarrels are not allowed to grow.

The smaller quarrels are an outburst due to tension

in our lives. They pass off as the tension is released and these can even bind a couple together. However, when differences are allowed to grow in silence, and with an indifferent attitude, the tension piles up and can cripple the relationship. Some day the pent-up tension is released in a sudden explosion. This may break the marriage. Many times these quarrels are ignored in the hope that better sense will prevail upon the partner. However, this does not happen.

The real solution lies in resolving differences as they arise. Daily tensions must not be allowed to fester. Find an outlet for them through a small quarrel, an argument, some form of recreation, or through a well-adjusted sex life. Do not let these tensions accumulate. Learn to understand each other's grievances effectively. Find solutions acceptable to both to keep the marriage alive and happy.

Life is What You Make

The ultimate success of marriage depends as much upon the husband as on the wife. Your wife may not be the finest person in the world, but neither are you. Everyone has good and bad qualities. If you want your needs to be fulfilled, you will have to fulfil your wife's needs.

A woman spends a considerable amount of time within the precincts of the home, bringing up the children, and building a home where the whole family retires each evening to find comfort and peace.

It is a never-ending task and can be very trying sometimes. Give her due consideration for that. You may be doing your fair share by providing for the whole family, but never put your married life on a scale where you give for what you receive from the family. Learn to give as much of yourself as you can and you shall find everlasting happiness.

Points to Ponder

❖ Your wife is the most important woman in your life.

❖ Understand love. Understand your wife's need for love.

❖ A good marriage is a two-way relationship.

❖ Develop a mutually satisfying relationship.

❖ Money can create differences in marriage.

❖ Do not overlook marital problems. Solve them.

❖ Be fair in love and marriage.

❖ Life is what you make it.

■ ■

2. Your Children

"The first duty to children is to make them happy. If you have not made them so, you have wronged them. No other good they may get can make up for that."

–Buxton

There is a desire in each of us to renew ourselves through our children. We want them to be like us, to be what we think we stand for in life. Yet, to the displeasure of many parents, children grow up to be something quite different, frustrating many hopes and aspirations. Parents then begin to wonder what could have gone wrong and when and where. But, invariably, it is too late to make amends.

What children grow up to be is not a matter of chance. Parents who are directly responsible for their upbringing may act without consciously being aware of it, but through their daily actions, they influence the child's future. Most parents will insist that what they do for their children is the best under the circumstances. The shortcomings in upbringing are due to variations in perception and the execution of basic needs of childcare. This, in turn, depends upon one's basic knowledge about the subject.

The Child's Needs

The basic needs of a child to enable him to grow up into a responsible adult will vary from age to age. As an infant, the needs are restricted to being nourished, kept clean, warm and well protected. However, as he grows up to gain awareness of the people and the environment around him, he begins to form impressions and memories that could appreciably make or mar his adult life. Just as proper nourishment, cleanliness and a good education are important, so are his needs for love, affection and security, which he needs to develop self-confidence.

He must have a rich storehouse of memories from which he can draw in adult life. These cannot all be provided at one time. They have to be infused day after day in doses he can conveniently assimilate. This may be a tall order in today's competitive times. It is here that a happy home is a valuable asset. In a congenial atmosphere, a father and mother can provide these needs almost effortlessly, if they understand their role in the child's upbringing.

The Father's Role

For most fathers, their duty is well performed if they can provide a reasonably good education and a decent standard of living for their children. To them, good education means sending the child to a good school and later to college. A good standard of living means providing the usual needs of food, clothes and shelter, with an occasional pampering with presents that may be anything from a chocolate to a new toy, or perhaps an expensive set of clothes. This pattern of living may be flavoured with an outing or a holiday occasionally. A few fathers may occasionally help in baby-sitting. Beyond this, most men hardly feel the need for involvement in the child's upbringing until much later, when they find that the child is not growing up to be what they had desired.

Whereas it is true that a mother has a greater role to play in the child's upbringing during infancy, the father's role is no less important. Modern society is such that much of a man's time is spent away from home, in his struggle to eke out a living. Yet, in the short time available to him, there is much that a father can do for his children.

A child looks up to his father as a pillar of strength, as a symbol of righteousness and godliness. He knows him to be a person who has answers to all his questions. This places a heavy responsibility on any father. If he wants to enjoy the confidence and respect of the family, he will have to live up to these high expectations. With the demands for more freedom by women, and a general awareness of their rights, men will need to share more responsibilities at home. This will require both knowledge and an effort in this direction.

The Growing Child

During infancy, the role of a father may be no more than that of a helpmate to his wife. As the child begins to sit, crawl and move about, and gains awareness about the world around him, the need for an active interest in his upbringing arises. The father's role cannot be delegated to another person. Not even to the mother.

From the age of three onwards the child begins to get emotionally attached to the parents. Daughters have a strong attachment to fathers and their childhood experiences may influence their selection of a husband in future. The daughter's married life too will be influenced by her childhood memories.

In the same way, although a boy is more attached to the mother, he begins to identify himself with his father. The children take their father's surname and every man desires that his children follow his footsteps. A good school will bear the responsibility of teaching the child the three Rs, but the home will be the main place where he will learn some of the most important things about life and living.

A Happy Childhood

This is the greatest gift a parent can give children. Happiness does not mean a pampered life with all that money can buy, but a life rich in pleasant memories. No other factor exerts greater influence on adult habits and attitudes as childhood memories do. In times of distress, adults draw great strength from their childhood experiences and are able to cross hurdles easily.

Let your child have fine memories to grow up with. Give him your time, love and understanding, and do it patiently. Let him feel that you care. Some of the finest things a person remembers were conveyed to him in childhood through bedtime stories narrated by the father or mother. Storytelling is a medium with unlimited possibilities. Some of the most intricate values have been imparted to children through the pleasant experiences of these stories. If you can instil in the mind of your child a vision to view the future with hope and courage, you have given him a wonderful tool to level out the problems of adult life. Such a vision grows out of experiences based on emotions such as love, kindness, sympathy, generosity and thoughtfulness.

Habits for a Lifetime

Any action performed repeatedly becomes a habit. Our actions, in turn, depend upon thoughts. Through positive thoughts and suggestions, parents can turn a child into a confident adult who is able to use his full capabilities. However, if the suggestions are not intelligent, or based on wrong knowledge, they can teach the child wrong values, marring his chances of success forever.

Of course, no parent would like his child to form habits that would be detrimental to his future. Most parents leave their children to receive these all-important suggestions from the general environments in which they live and do not contribute as much as they should, particularly in the earlier stages, when children are the most impressionable. The results, therefore, are far from encouraging. This makes it necessary that the parents make an early and deliberate effort to ensure that the child develops good habits.

Great strength comes from an orderly and systematic way of life. A child will at times oppose what you tell him to do. This is only because he wishes to test the limits. Do not let this discourage you. Until he can accept the ways you suggest, there will be a great need for patience and tolerance on the part of both mother and father. There are many good habits that need to be imparted on vital subjects like eating, health, work and rest, success and failure, and how to get along amiably with others.

During training, parents are often perturbed over the level of intelligence of their child. They connect everything he says, or does, as a reflection of his intelligence in later life. This is not always true. It does not matter how soon a child begins to teeth, or learns to sit, crawl or walk; nor does it matter if he is slow to learn how to speak clearly. There are significant variations in such matters. He may need special attention in exceptional cases only. Provided the child is visibly healthy and maintains steady growth, one need not be anxious about such matters. Even the slowest of children have grown up to be perfectly normal adults.

A child is extremely observant and attaches great significance even to what may appear quite trifling to adults. It is in these early years of life that a person learns to accept or reject the principles of truth, honesty and selflessness. A child does not know what is good for him and what is not. He learns from what he sees. His environment shapes his actions and moulds his habits for a lifetime.

Developing the Child's Self-confidence

It is unfortunate that parents will send their children to the best schools and colleges, but do not prepare them to develop self-confidence. Thereby, they do not prepare them to face the challenges of life. Most parents would be happier if this too could form a part of the regular educational curriculum. However, self-confidence is an asset for a lifetime and all parents will do well to train their children in this.

SECTION-III

A child cannot develop confidence overnight. It comes gradually from small successes achieved from time to time. Every success builds him to face a bigger challenge. The accumulated effect of these successes prepares him to face the struggles of daily life in adulthood.

A factor that can rob a child of self-confidence is fear of various kinds. He may be afraid of darkness, of having strange people around and the like. Many parents do a lot of harm by instilling imaginary fears in the child's mind so as to frighten him into being more disciplined. In the same way, many mothers instil an image of severe authority to represent what a father means to the child. Such thoughts can become a part of the person for a lifetime. One of the first lessons in developing his confidence must be in teaching him to differentiate between real and imaginary fears. Knowledge helps dispel unnecessary fears.

Positive encouragement is a sure way to help the child develop self-confidence. Children like to be appreciated for what they do and attach particular importance to the qualities for which they are specially appreciated and encouraged. Even in school, children give special attention to subjects in which they score better. Initially, the unconscious encouragement they might have received sets them making special efforts in a particular direction. However, it is necessary to understand that encouragement and flattery are not the same thing. Encouragement must be sincere and a useful guide that the child can rely upon.

Help the child develop a wide range of interests and build lasting friendships. The more he understands about human nature in early life, the better his prospects of accepting human problems of adulthood as a part of normal life. What parents specially need to understand is that the world is predominantly inhabited by people governed by negative thoughts. Most people see the darker rather than the brighter side of life. If the child is allowed to grow up under such influences, it will only stifle his imagination forever, robbing him of his confidence for life.

Children have their own way of interpreting facts. To exercise their imagination they will put forward viewpoints that can be very different from established values. No intelligent parent should condemn these views without giving them a fair hearing. Even when you have to turn down a child's views, do this tactfully. Give him your reasons for this. Do not kill his initiative. You should not give him the impression that you do not care. Children can be very sensitive about such things.

Winning the Child's Confidence

To ensure that your training is well accepted, you will need to build the child's confidence in yourself. This can be one of the finest assets with which you can capably guide him towards independence.

Children will be curious. Do not brush off their curiosity as irritating or ridiculous. Answer their questions as best as you can. Do not tell them something that you know is not true. Eventually, every child comes to know the truth and he may lose confidence in whatever you tell him.

An important factor that robs the child's confidence in parents is when they do not practise what they preach. Unfortunately, too many of us have dual standards. Many parents rationalise this by saying that while they want their children to learn what is best for them, they can themselves break the rules since they can differentiate between good and bad. No child appreciates such an attitude. Children learn their parents' standards and if parents cannot be honest with children, there is no reason why they should expect children to be honest with them.

Patience and tact can be your never-failing tools to win him over. When you respect his feelings, he will respect yours. Loving care always pays huge dividends. When you treat him as an individual and do not insist that he should be what you want him to be, he will confide in you.

The Value of Money

The correct values about money must be taught to children at an early stage. They must know that money is a medium of exchange for labour. To gain it one must give something of equal value. Perhaps they may not need to contribute physically as parents do. However, even in early stages, a child must know that to earn his pocket money he needs to devote labour to studying wholeheartedly in school and, later, by helping his parents at home. A child must understand that before he can desire a thing, he must be willing to work for it.

To teach children about money, let them handle money. Their first lessons can begin with the weekly allowance, or pocket money, they may receive from you. Give increments as they grow. When they handle money, they can be taught the need for honesty in their dealings, the need to maintain accounts and keep track of their money. A common problem at this stage is how much a child should get as pocket money. This depends partly upon the financial circumstances of the parents, and partly on the type of school he studies in, reflecting that level of society.

At this stage, the child can also be told about the need for saving some money for future use. They can be told how the little coins they collect can gradually be amassed into larger sums. Many banks now offer schemes to encourage savings amongst children, and operate accounts for minor children.

As children grow up, they will like to take interest in the running of the home. They may like to know how much is spent on what. It may also be worthwhile to tell them why they can have one thing and not another. By running little errands in making purchases for the home, they can be taught how to spend money intelligently to get its full worth. They will make mistakes, but this is the only practical way to learn. Through these lessons, you will be preparing them to boldly face the bigger challenges of life.

Punishing the Child

At times, to enforce discipline, a child will need to be punished. This is of special significance to a father as many children look up to their fathers with fear and awe, as mothers often instil a picture of the father being an unquestioned authority. But a father should take care that he is looked upon as a friend and guide, and not just as a punishing force.

Punishment is intended to make a child aware of the need for some discipline and not as a source of inflicting physical or emotional injury. Each child being different, no set form of punishment is good enough each time. At one time, a scolding is all that may be necessary. On another occasion, one may need to be more severe. Whatever punishment you may impose, under no circumstances should your sense of fairness be challenged. The child must understand that he has done something undesirable and therefore the need for punishment. If he realises his mistake, you could even ask him to suggest the punishment. Teach him to own up his fault and be repentant about it. Be firm, but understanding.

Many parents confuse punishment and insults as the same thing. They are not. Do punish him if he deserves it, but do not insult him, particularly when others are around. He will retaliate, declare you unfair, and lose confidence in your sense of justice. Give the child every opportunity to explain his point of view. Distract him from what is bad with love, tact and patience rather than with force and authority. The punishment should keep him away from what is bad, not from you!

Teaching About Sex

Sex is no longer as mysterious as it used to be. Children come across all sorts of advertisements on the road, in magazines and even on radio and television. Eventually, they will want to know more about sex. If they have confidence in their parents, they will obviously be the first choice for questions. However, if their curiosity is brushed aside, they will turn to knowledgeable friends. Brushing aside the child's inquiry may be less embarrassing, but since the knowledge he may collect from his friends may be misleading and harmful, it is imperative that parents impart this knowledge themselves.

Sex information can be imparted gradually at different stages. In early childhood, the minor questions can be answered briefly to banish doubts. You will need to use your imagination for this. If you can explain things clearly, you can be certain that the child's knowledge is based upon facts and not on hearsay. When the child grows up, there will be the need for the father to explain things to the son, and the mother could explain them to the daughter. It is necessary that the knowledge the parents impart is factual and unbiased.

Adolescence

The period when a child passes from childhood to manhood or womanhood is termed as adolescence. This can be a very trying period for the child. He undergoes such rapid physical and emotional changes, it becomes difficult to get used to them quickly. The growing child can neither identify himself amongst children, nor with adults. He may become extremely self-conscious, nervous and irritable, and may desire to be left alone. While externally he may try to appear self-sufficient, inwardly he will desire to be loved and guided. He becomes especially conscious of the opposite sex, but will want to hide his feelings. There may be an occasional argument, a desire to flout authority as a mark of having grown up, but invariably each spell ends up with remorse.

This is a significant period in character formation and there will be the need to be firm and understanding. It can be to your advantage if you have already won the confidence of the child. You will need to be watchful and reassure him that you understand his problems. He may insist his problems are unique. With understanding parents, things become easier for the child. What you need to impress upon him is that nature is preparing him for adult life and, in due course of time, he will be ready to live independently.

Preparing for Independence

As young people move out of the home to pursue further studies, or a career, their interests grow in varied activities and, simultaneously, they move slightly away from the parents. Despite self-confidence, the youth will continue to need guidance about several things.

A growing interest in the opposite sex will present the problem of explaining in more detail about love, sex and marriage. Each generation has a lot to say about these vital issues. Parents who accept this as normal will continue to enjoy the confidence of their children.

Likewise, there will be the need to advise them about the selection of a partner for marriage and about settling down in life.

After marriage, the interest of the son or daughter will be diverted towards the partner. Do not let this bother you. This does not mean that their love for you has waned. They have now grown up to a stage when they will need to attend to many details to live independently. If you have sincerely given them your love and guidance, they will continue to return this in many forms. Learn to live graciously under the changed circumstances and watch your children prosper.

Points to Ponder

- ❖ We renew our lives through our children.
- ❖ All children need loving care to grow up into responsible adults.
- ❖ A father's role in the child's upbringing is no less important than a mother's role.
- ❖ A happy childhood is the best gift you can give your child.
- ❖ A balanced adult life depends upon happy childhood memories.
- ❖ Habits for a lifetime are formed in childhood.
- ❖ Win the child's confidence. It makes communication easy and effective.
- ❖ Money values are best learnt in childhood.
- ❖ Adolescents need parental guidance and support.
- ❖ Caring parents help children step into independent adult life confidently.

■ ■

AT WORK

Every person who has his sights on top positions devotes his best efforts to his work. To most people, work is the first priority in life. They follow work so zealously that it is not long before other commitments in life get out of balance. The materialistic society in which we live only motivates them to strive harder, whatever the cost. Stress then builds up. There could be a rapid burnout. Family responsibilities are affected. Society begins to change its attitude. Even the work begins to suffer.

Should it be that way? Not at all! Certainly not for the complete man! A balanced life is the first priority for the complete man. There must be balance between his commitments to the wife and family, his work and responsibilities towards society. Work is an essential part of one's life. We need to work to get what we need. However, this should not be at the cost of other commitments.

The present generation is more fortunate compared to their predecessors. They have more knowledge at their command than ever before. An essential element of this knowledge is that one needs to work smarter, not harder. Experts in every field have helped provide knowledge on how to live a successful life. Psychologists have given greater insights into the human mind. This helps in building better relationships. Greater success is now possible at work. There are more efficiency aids than ever before. Opportunities abound for individuals to become more productive.

At work, it was never easier to become the complete man.

1. Attaining Success

"The greatest results in life are usually attained by simple means and the exercise of ordinary qualities. These may for the most part be summed in these two words – common sense and perseverance."

–Feltham

All successful people have believed in and followed certain simple rules of living to make success their constant companion. These successful people have not reached great heights because they were more fortunate than others and had luck on their side. For them to wait for luck to smile would have been like waiting for the impossible to happen, closing one's eyes to facts and wasting some of the best years of their lives. The truth is they had mastered the art of success.

The wonderful world of success is open to all who are willing to make the effort to learn the rules that take one towards the goal. It is for all those who believe in them, and practise them until they become a part of life.

What is Success?

Is success having lots of money? A luxurious home? A new car? Fame? A title? Many friends? Yes, success could be one of these things or all of them, depending on one's personal outlook. Many people have acquired these things and even more. Yet, others may not be willing to call them successful.

For the complete man, a person is successful when he can realise himself through it. For him, to be successful means to live up to what he expects from himself. He must find personal satisfaction in it. His success must be compatible with his inner self. It must be balanced in the various spheres of life. Only when a man can enjoy being alive, and likes all that is around him, can he be said to be truly successful.

Success does not come from hard work alone. People have laboured all their lives, yet lived in poverty. Nor does it come from having lots of money. People have inherited and earned lots of money, yet never found it worthwhile. Money is a means to an end, not an end in itself. Success comes only from realisation of personal goals and living a balanced life.

Opportunities for Success

Opportunities abound all around us. Few avail of them. What exactly does one mean by the word 'opportunity'? Is it a mysterious force that comes knocking at the doors of a blessed few? Is it the power to push and pull through life with the recommendations of friends and relatives? Perhaps to some it means a tailor-made job, a flourishing business handed down from the family, or winning the jackpot. If an opportunity is one of these things, then yes, opportunities are getting scarce.

Opportunities do not come. They have to be created. An opportunity is no more than a fragment of a thought that comes floating into the mind. We toy around with it. Through it we view a vision, shape it with hard work, and gradually turn the dream into reality.

Contrary to common belief, opportunities are not scarce. They are constantly growing manifold. Each time a new discovery is made, or an invention perfected, it does not mean that yet another opportunity is closed. It means that many new opportunities are opening by way of jobs. Human beings have unlimited needs and as long as there is a single human being on this earth, with needs to fulfil, there will be opportunities to fulfil them.

Self-evaluation for Success

As we start our journey towards more successful living, we need to look back on our past successes, personal aptitudes and capabilities. We need to organise what we have. And make up for what we lack.

In making a personal assessment of yourself, be realistic, not idealistic. Too many of us try to rationalise our shortcomings rather than admit them. So above all else, be truthful to yourself. You may be tempted to cheat others about yourself, but it never pays to cheat oneself.

Look back at your education, parental influence and the environment you have grown up in. Do you feel they have contributed towards personal success? Alternatively, have they let you down many a time? How is your health? Good, bad, or indifferent? Have you any areas of emotional conflict?

A happy childhood and youth are good stepping-stones to success. Happy memories promote self-confidence and faith in people who matter. However, the majority look back at unfulfilled desires, wishing that circumstances were more kind. We cannot choose our parents, and only a few are capable of controlling the environment in their childhood. Besides, nothing can be done about the time gone by. By allowing unhappy thoughts about the past to linger on, you are robbing yourself of vital strength that can help you in the future. Forget the past.

Do not let the thought that you are too young or too old for success hold you back. Age is not important. Each one of us is constantly changing, gradually dropping some qualities and developing others. Whether this is for the better depends upon how conscientious we are in developing good habits. Both young and old have brought about great things in life. With the correct mental attitude, so can you.

To prepare yourself for success in the near future,

you will need to evaluate your aptitudes. We like certain activities more than others do. These preferences can be traced back to parental influence; to the encouragement we might have received from those whom we met in life. What is important is that we have better chances of success if we adopt them as a part of our life. The shortest route to success is to develop those qualities and pursue those activities that have contributed to earlier success.

To understand this better, write down your past achievements. Against each achievement note down qualities that contributed towards each success. In the same way, note down instances when you failed to achieve what you had set out to do. Again, note down bad qualities that betrayed you. You would now have a list of both your good and bad points. Then, it is only a matter of developing your strong points, and gradually overcoming your weaknesses.

With your past successes and failures in black and white before you, you will begin to realise why it is important to cultivate habits like self-control, tact and understanding, moderation in everything, positive thinking, being soft-spoken, and being thoughtful about others. All these virtues contribute to build a good character, helping develop power from within. With bad habits like carelessness, procrastination, indifference towards others and negligence gradually eliminated from daily living, one is able to take full advantage of one's efforts towards more successful living.

Success Consciousness

It does not matter whether you are looking forward to building a house, starting an industrial venture, standing for the general elections, or just planning a meeting of a group of friends to discuss an important issue. Before success can be achieved in real life, it must become a reality in your mind. A thought is a powerful force and if one must make success a constant companion, every force must be put into action.

To be successful, you must be consciously aware of your ability to be capable of it not once, but every time. This self-confidence keeps generating a powerful force within a person. With success achieved mentally, each time one gets into action, there is not only an advantage over others, but success comes almost automatically.

How do you rate yourself on success? Do you only wish this or genuinely desire it? If you only wish it, you are unconsciously admitting that you are not capable of it. If it must come, then it can come only as a gift from heaven. However, when you desire it, and believe in your ability to achieve it, you have placed a goal before yourself. The power generated from the belief in your ability will positively help you reach there.

As the intensity of the desire to reach a particular goal increases, the mind too accelerates its search for ways and means to fulfil the desire. The more you feed the mind with optimistic thoughts, the closer you get to success. With each success, your success consciousness grows. You begin to qualify for a glorious victory every time.

Setting Targets

You cannot expect to reach your destination unless you know where exactly you desire to go. If you keep working in the hope that one day you might be able to crystallise your dreams into reality, you are no better than the sailor who is hoping to reach a treasure island by allowing the waves to carry him wherever they go.

Define your targets clearly. Write down exactly what you desire. Then set deadlines to achieve it. One cannot climb up the ladder in a single leap. While setting deadlines, you can break up the main target into smaller sections, and set dates for achieving each. The short-term targets will give you an opportunity to climb up rung-by-rung, enable you to evaluate the success from time to time and, if necessary, adopt measures to deal with setbacks you encounter. Some people set themselves targets for the day each morning. They make certain that they attain them by the evening. However, no fixed rules can be made for such things. Each person can decide as to what suits him.

In setting targets, be realistic about your capabilities. When a person sets out to achieve more than he can handle, it is easy for him to get disheartened and give up altogether.

You should remember that nothing could be achieved unless one is willing to give something of equal value in return. All successful men have achieved success through giving a part of themselves through service to humanity in general. The plant breeder achieves success for the new varieties he has produced, the manufacturer for giving better products at a lesser price, the lawyer for the legal protection he offers, and so on. You too can give a part of yourself at home, at your work, and in your social life. What you achieve will be in proportion to what you give. There can be no success without it.

A Plan of Action
Nobody who has an objective to achieve within a set time can wait for inspiration to get going. A certain amount of work must be done regularly. Success cannot come out of haphazard work. You will need to formulate a plan of action. It should be in keeping with your health and personal capabilities. It should allow you to work with a singleness of purpose. It must define time for work and time for relaxation and leisure.

A certain amount of knowledge is essential to achieve any objective. If you have it, well and good. If you do not, then you may like to acquire it. In case that is not possible immediately, you will need the assistance of someone who does have the requisite knowledge. You may also need to build a library of information that may be required from time to time. This is important because not everything can be remembered. Even if one does try to fill the mind with information that may be required only occasionally, one may end up with a confused state of mind. Instead, it is preferable to learn how to maintain and get pertinent information whenever it may be required.

Be Creative

With the desire to achieve one's goals in life growing, a man begins to search for ways and means to achieve them. One of the finest sources of great power is one's own creative power. Everyone has it, but few know how to develop or use it. Once one learns to put this wonderful power within us to use, it works like a fountain of new ideas.

Creativity grows with successful living. Learn to be happy, to be at ease, physically and emotionally. As one concentrates on areas of success, self-confidence grows and creativity blossoms. All ideas start as a little thought. Toy around with it in the mind. Let imagination do its work. Analyse the ideas. Investigate their utility. Let them crystallise into a plan. Then execute it into reality.

To get a regular supply of creative thoughts, keep your subconscious mind busy. Use it to advantage as often as you can. It is like any other power. The more you use it, the better and more reliable it becomes. Use it to create opportunities for success and for personal promotion in life.

Dare to be Different

If it had not been for people who dared to be different, we might still have been living in the Stone Age. All progress has come about because there were people who wanted to venture into the unknown. In addition, for their daring, they were amply rewarded through public recognition and material benefits – both symbols of success.

A certain amount of profit comes from the risk a

person takes in any enterprise. By refusing to take the risk, you are expressing your inability to back your own thinking with action. You doubt your own ability to succeed. This does not mean that you should plunge into a venture just because there can be no profit without a certain amount of risk. Not all risks are the same. Calculate your risks. Once you are satisfied that more odds are in your favour, do not let the fear of being different hold you back.

If you feel that quitting your job and joining a more progressive company will bring you faster success, do go ahead. If you feel it will be advantageous to close down an age-old business and start another one, do go ahead. Likewise with everything else. Try a new décor in your home, offer a new type of service in your business, or plan a different kind of a programme in your club. Then prove that you can make a success of each of them.

The Need for Action

The desire to win, acquisition of knowledge, and developing new and better ideas are wonderful ingredients to achieve success, but none of them are of any use until they are put into action. Real, live action!

It does not matter whether you desire to serve society by becoming a schoolteacher, a workshop manager, a salesman or a company director. You cannot succeed unless you act. It is at this stage that many people fall out from reaching the ultimate goal. They had all that it required to be a success. Yet, they failed because they did not know how to put their plans into action. Why?

The fault lies in their personal attitudes. They lack self-confidence. They are afraid of criticism and failure. They have not developed sufficient success consciousness in their minds. They are constantly weighed down by various fears.

If you too are a victim of such fears, now is the time to change your outlook. Study the pros and cons of your thoughts and ideas, but do not let indecision hold you back. To be a success, you must act.

Taking Decisions

This is not half as difficult as most people imagine it to be. It is a matter of experience. Those who have learnt this wonderful art are amongst the highest paid and most respected people in the world.

In decision-making there are 50 per cent chances that you are right and 50 per cent that you are not. However, if you avoid taking a decision altogether, the chances are that you will always be wrong. Besides, you will unconsciously be acquiring the harmful habit of indecisiveness – one of the greatest obstacles to successful living. Indecision is a negative decision. It is the hallmark of the inefficient and the irresponsible.

To arrive at a decision, follow this simple procedure. Write each detail on paper until you can learn to do it swiftly in your mind:

1. Define the problem clearly.
2. Collect facts from as many sources as possible.
3. Study the pros and cons calmly. Do not let anyone force you into a decision.
4. Make an appropriate decision.

Nobody can make a correct decision every time. If you are wrong, admit it. Do not justify it.

Concentration at Work

Success comes from a serious effort to achieve what you have set out to do. When at it, put aside other thoughts. You will not like to reduce the force you are applying on the target at hand. Why divide your attention and efforts on more than one target? Arrange your work so that there will be the least amount of interruption from others.

Concentrate on one thing at a time. Thereby, you will remove all external influences from disturbing the flow of energy and productivity in the subconscious mind.

You will be able to draw on the mind's vast reservoir of information, organising it to a form useful to you. This way, solutions to some of the most difficult problems are easily found.

Enjoy Your Work

Unfortunately, too many people hate the idea of going to work. To them, it is truly going to 'the daily grind'. However, the complete man looks forward to it as a personal challenge to help him grow. What makes it arduous or enjoyable is not the work itself, but the attitude of the person doing it. All work is the same. It is for you to accept it mentally as interesting or as boring.

When you like your work, you are not only going to enjoy doing it but you will also do it much better – quantitatively and qualitatively. When you enjoy what you do, there is no scope for symptoms of fatigue to set in and rob you of efficiency.

The Art of Self-motivation

Sometimes our minds are extremely sharp and there is a continuous and effortless flow of useful ideas. Similarly, there are other times when we are highly productive in that we are able to do a lot of work without the slightest sign of monotony, boredom or fatigue. Some describe this enhanced activity as inspiration – a divine influence making the work effortless. Such occasions are rare. We cannot wait for inspiration to control our daily activities.

People perform better if their minds are stimulated in a specific manner. The response to a particular form of stimulation is the same each time. However, different people respond differently to varied stimuli. Some are inspired by praise and honour; some by music; others by the serenity of nature in a garden, and yet others by someone they love dearly. Each time people are exposed to their favourite form of stimulation, they become highly creative and productive.

You too can capitalise on this fact by finding out what stimulates you. Listen to the music you like, visit places that interest you or meet people who inspire you. Create the type of environment that suits you. Learn to motivate yourself into activity by thinking of the many rewards that await you. In this manner you can tap your entire productive powers all the time.

Keep Improving

As our experience in life grows, we begin to realise how much there is to learn. Knowledge in all fields of activities is growing so rapidly that a person who ignores it risks being left behind in this competitive world. It is essential to set aside a period for self-improvement. This time can be utilised to learn and to put into action new ideas that may help you in understanding yourself better or in taking you closer to your goals.

You can gain a lot by being in the company of the learned. There are several other sources of knowledge too. Postal courses, short-term refresher courses, trade and business journals, newspapers and a range of magazines on varied subjects can regularly offer you ideas for self-improvement, stimulating your creativity.

Don't be Easily Satisfied

Set higher targets at work. Make each time better than the last. Keep reminding yourself that there must be a better and a cheaper way of doing the job.

While writing a letter, ask yourself if you have used the best paper, printed a neat and impressive letterhead, and written it without any errors. If you are running a factory, are you certain that production cannot be increased or wastage reduced? If you own a general store, are you sure you are rendering the best possible service to customers?

Whatever your present level of success, remember that there is always scope for improvement. Render a little more service than what you are paid for. The more you give the better will be your returns in the days to come.

Perseverance Pays

Too often, long after an opportunity has gone, we realise that we failed to reach our goal because we stopped a few steps short. The road to success is long and tiring. It entails work, more work, and still more work. It is for you to find ways to make the journey to success more interesting to keep you going. If you want to reach your destination, you will have to keep going. Too many fortunes were lost when someone could not keep up with the struggle. Surely, you would not like to do the same?

During the journey, do not let obstacles discourage you. Enthusiasm is your greatest asset. It can keep you moving towards your goals. Keep charging yourself with renewed enthusiasm and thoughts of success and keep working till you succeed.

Integrity, Honour and Truth

Somewhere along your journey, you will come to a point where the road forks into two distinct paths. On the one hand, you see the more rugged path, interspersed with obstacles, discouragement, and perhaps even temporary defeat, but you know that it surely leads to your goal. On the other hand, there is the apparently smooth highway which promises an easy journey, but with some uncertainty.

Beware – do not be tempted into hurried decisions. The first path is that of integrity, honour and truth. Although it appears difficult, ultimately, it is the only sure path. The second path may appear swift and pleasant, and promise quicker returns, but in reality it can lead only to shame and dishonour.

Temptations come to test people in strange ways. One mistake and a person may be doomed for life. However difficult the path of virtue appears, do not forsake it. It is the only path to real success. It may take you a lot of time, but never compromise with factors that affect your character. The loss in intangible forms can be manifold. Man loses his peace of mind, happiness, and a chance for real success forever.

Help Others

In helping others succeed, you gain substantial success yourself. Be they your friends or subordinates, help them to achieve success in what is dear to them, help them satisfy their personal needs.

This way you benefit two-fold. Firstly, as you guide them to achieve what they desire, you are mentally repeating and accepting the simple rules of success, thus fortifying your faith in yourself. Secondly, as those whom you guide achieve success in their efforts, they cannot help using their might to help you in return. They would always want you to succeed in your ventures because in a way their success depends upon you.

Promote Yourself

If you are a good worker and do your duty well, it is not enough. Others must be aware of your capabilities also. You cannot promote yourself without it. This does not mean that you should go about telling everyone that you are an excellent worker. If you do this, others may consider you proud and boastful. Rather than appreciate your work, they may try to lower you in others' esteem.

However, you should not shun the credit due to you. The next time there is a business meeting, do not take a rear seat. Sit where people can see you. Do not hesitate to give your candid opinions. Suggest improvements that can be incorporated in the working of your department in particular and the company in general.

When you take a problem to an immediate superior, clearly state your own inferences and possible solutions. The chances are that one of the solutions suggested by you may be accepted, improving your boss's estimation of your ability. In the same way, if you are preparing a report on the workings of your company, do not be satisfied by putting together the data asked for. See if the information can be supplemented with ideas to promote the cause.

If you have a positive idea about improving the organisation, do not keep it to yourself. Pass this on to the appropriate authorities. Tell them who can benefit from these suggestions. This way you can gradually gain a lot of peer approval.

Each one of us is expected to do a certain amount of work as part of our normal duties. If we can do a little more than what is expected of us, we will be telling all concerned that we are capable of more responsibility. These little extras keep one well ahead of the competition.

Handling Criticism

There are two kinds of people. Those who work hard to achieve success. And those who try to bring others down with criticism to gain the consolation that they are no less important. The latter are those who are not sufficiently enthusiastic to work sincerely. Their only response to the success achieved by others is to criticise and bring them down.

Severe criticism can be a major obstacle in the path to success. However, if you wish to achieve your goals in life, you will have to learn to take it patiently. Do not let criticism discourage you from moving on towards your goals. Criticism is often useful as it keeps one alert and helps plug loopholes that may have been overlooked. It gives you a chance to be meticulous in everything you do.

The limelight is always focused on people who make success a constant companion. Quite often even minor shortcomings begin to appear unduly magnified from the viewer's angle. Nobody is perfect. Therefore, do not let criticism upset you. It is just a part of being successful.

Defeat and Failure

Everyone is liable to make mistakes. These can mean a setback to one's progress, which can be discouraging. If people were to accept this simple fact, many more would succeed in their efforts. Unfortunately, these setbacks are too much to bear for most people. It is not long before they succumb to their failings and resign themselves to failure.

If there were no obstacles, few would appreciate those who reach the top. We can call a thing good because we can differentiate it from what is bad. In the same way, riches are conspicuous after one has seen poverty. Likewise, if we have seen defeat, we value success more.

A defeat is a temporary setback. To be successful, anticipate setbacks. Anticipate temporary defeats. They are a part of our journey towards success. Use every setback as a springboard to take a bigger leap into the onward journey. Look at it from a positive angle. The more the setbacks one has to face, the more one knows of things that do not work. This knowledge is what we call experience. It has to be gained by actually going through it. There is no other way.

More Problems Along the Way

Along the journey, you are likely to encounter other problems too. You need to understand that these are part of normal life. They should not arouse undue anxiety. To know about them is to be prepared to tackle them when they arise. Although many set out to achieve success, there are many dropouts at every stage. Barely five per cent make it to the mark.

Procrastination is one problem that can seriously affect progress. Avoid it. Another problem is when we overestimate our progress. Our eagerness to move on fools us into believing that we are moving faster than we actually do. This can be misleading, creating complacency, which can retard further progress. It is essential that we take a realistic view, although it may hurt our vanity to be a trifle slow.

And there is the problem that can affect all ambitious men – success taking one away from home. Some of the greatest men have failed on this score. One will need to be careful about it. Too often, as a man drives towards success, he becomes so obsessed that he forgets his home and family. If success were to keep a man perennially away from home, it would be of little value. He might have the psychological satisfaction of having achieved what he wanted, but if this is at the cost of the family's happiness, it is too high a price to pay for personal success.

The solution to this problem is simple. Set a fair balance between your work and your home. While at one place you can earn material benefits, at the other you can enjoy them with your family. Either of them is useless without the other.

For the man who is in a hurry to climb the ladder of success, the demands of a family may appear an unnecessary distraction. This is not so. It is not just a fair deal for the family alone, but also for him. It gives him a chance to relax and prepare him for greater challenges in life. Time spent in a happy home is like recharging the battery of one's driving force, to have renewed vigour to keep on the journey to success the following day.

At the Top

As you begin to achieve what you set out to do, you will appreciate why it was important to discipline yourself, why you needed a plan of action, and how every little effort contributed towards reaching your destination. By now you will also become fully aware of what can positively help you and what cannot. Since every action repeatedly builds up into a habit, it should not be difficult for you to maintain the position you are capable of.

No successful man enjoys his success alone. His family should be a partner in it, and even his friends and colleagues can enjoy it with him.

It is at this stage that one begins to feel the possession of a new power with unlimited potential. Used for the welfare of mankind, it continues to grow. Used only to satisfy selfish ends, it begins to diminish as negative thoughts and actions begin to act on it. Used intelligently it can help you reap bountiful harvests repeatedly.

Points to Ponder

- ❖ Understand success. What does it mean to you?
- ❖ Evaluate yourself for success. Opportunities exist all around.
- ❖ Success begins by developing consciousness of success.
- ❖ Set targets. Prepare a plan of action.
- ❖ Put your creativity to work. Dare to be different.
- ❖ Act. Take decisions. Enjoy your work.
- ❖ Motivate yourself for success.
- ❖ Never be satisfied. Keep improving.
- ❖ Persevere. Be ethical. Help others.
- ❖ Face criticism boldly. Defeat is a stepping-stone to success.
- ❖ Problems come and go. Anticipate and face them boldly.
- ❖ Your place is at the top. Make success a habit.

■■

2. Life at the Workplace

"You may fool all the people some of the time and some of the people all the time, but you cannot fool all the people all the time."

–Abraham Lincoln

One of life's greatest challenges is to be able to get along well with people. Be it at home, office or in society, the man who can get along with others is the one to make a mark. People, in general, decide what is good for them and what is not. Therefore, we accept them as the most reliable of judges. We seek their approval and appreciation in many ways.

Man is gregarious by nature and he cannot do without people and their approval. Since the vast multitude set out simultaneously to achieve this selfish end without knowledge of what they need to give in return, the consequences are invariably unhappiness and human discord. Hopes turn into frustrations and the sensitive man begins to avoid people.

The ability to get along well with people has identified the great leaders of all times. To some, it comes naturally. Those who were not blessed with this precious gift persevered to study and unravel the mysteries of human behaviour. They tried to understand what people desired to place their confidence in them.

The knowledge of good human relations comes from keen observation and a special perception to understand correct human behaviour. This knowledge cannot be passed. Each one needs to go through the process of learning. It can become a useful part of oneself only after it is tried and tested in daily life. With experience, one learns to get along well with people.

People and Stress

Although initial contact with most people is often stimulating, to some degree it also causes anxiety and stress. In dealing with some people, the stress builds faster. But there are others who are impervious to such stress and find their relationships with others rather interesting. Some can be extra sensitive and avoid dealing with people. Both kinds have their advantages and disadvantages. People adjust their dealings to find the maximum satisfaction from it. They avoid those who make them tense. This is important because stress can be detrimental to health and may steal many years of useful life.

Fretting and fuming, as a means of coping with this form of stress, is useless. It can only make the situation worse. The solution lies in developing a positive attitude towards people. There is no such thing as perfect people. We are not perfect. So how can we expect others to be so? We need to accept them as they are and not as what we want them to be. It would be to our advantage to learn why they behave as they do. What forces motivate them to good or bad actions? Can we take advantage of these influences?

Perhaps we can. Before we can do so, we must understand them better.

The Benefits of Harmony

Since we cannot totally do away with dealing with people, the best solution lies in learning to understand and interact with them. In accepting them as they are, we can surely find great mental peace. Our changed attitude can clear many of the conflicts that bother us everyday.

As we learn to accept people as they are, a new possibility takes shape. We can take advantage of what Napoleon Hill, the author of Law of Success, has described as the principle of the mastermind. According to him, when two or more people are in harmony to achieve a common goal, then each person is endowed with a power that is more than what either of them could wield independently. This explains some of the greatest successes made by people in all spheres of life.

For the complete man this opens possibilities of success at home, at work and in society. If we can achieve harmony with our associates, we can turn our ability to get along with people into a very vital force to bring about tremendous progress for ourselves and for others.

Understanding People

Looking at people from their viewpoint, each person is the most important one in the world. His name is the sweetest word that he can hear. Whatever position he may occupy in life, he does not like to be thought of as insignificant. He wants to be treated as a unique individual. His sentiments are very important to him. He expects everyone to respect them.

He has certain basic requirements to be satisfied. He wants to be healthy, have a home, a family, security of livelihood and a feeling that he is fulfilling a purpose in life. He likes to feel important and desires to be appreciated for all the good he is doing. He also feels that his problems are unique and that nobody could face them any better than him. He has a personal philosophy about life, and each time he will be emphatic about his viewpoint being the most authoritative. In short, this is how the average man feels about his life.

When we look back at the past of any individual, we find that from his personal point of view he is right. What any individual is today is the result of his inherited characteristics reacting with the environment in which he grew up. Since no two human beings are born with similar characteristics, his demand for being accepted as a unique person is reasonable and right. It is true that there has never been one like him, there isn't one today, nor will there ever be another like him.

If we differ and do not think as he does, we should not declare him wrong. He may be wrong, but what he says and does appears right to him. He has learnt it that way. If we know him to be wrong, from his point of view it is the people and the environment in which he grew up which should be blamed. After all, he learnt it as it was taught to him.

Only one out of every 20 people looks at life from a positive viewpoint. Negative thoughts predominate the lives of the other 19. Rather a high percentage, but it is true. Others who may perhaps be even less capable than they are dominate them. Their lives are ruled by fears of all descriptions – of criticism, of being ridiculed before others, of losing good health, a loved one, or perhaps money, of failing or death and a whole lot of other things. Most times these people indulge in fears unknown even to themselves.

If this is pointed out, they will refuse to admit that they have failed in life for the simple reason that their outlook is negatively oriented. On the other hand, they will be quick to rationalise their actions, blaming their failures on sheer bad luck. Unwilling to change, they continue to live the life of a slave of an invisible monster. They have not known a life that is free from such misplaced worries and do not know what they are missing.

To make things worse, this large number of negative people will, directly or indirectly, influence the lives of the coming generations. Therefore, life moves on in this manner. And the jaded perceptions of the vast majority are accepted as normal.

Winning People Over
To win people over to your way of thinking, honour what is dear to them. Make them feel important through sincere

appreciation. Remember their names. Remember that, like you, they too have a home and a family. They have their needs to feel secure and to be appreciated for what they contribute to society. To attract their attention, take interest in them. Listen to what they wish to say. Everyone has his hopes and aspirations. He wants to express them to seek approval from those who take an interest in him. This makes him feel rather important.

Be a patient listener rather than an eager speaker. The way you speak is perhaps the most important factor in winning people over to your way of thinking. To be one of them, speak in their language. Unless you are speaking to people whom you know to be learned, do not speak in a language that sounds too learned. People who act and speak in a superior way make others feel ignorant and inferior. Surely, you cannot expect a person to appreciate you if you are constantly reminding him that he is not as learned as you are! People can have very varied tastes, and if you want a large circle of friends who will like you, the need to talk in their language will require you to be well-versed in many subjects. A man who has a wide range of interests will always interest others.

Never indulge in gossip. It has never done anybody any good. It invariably starts with a casual remark about someone. Each time it is repeated, it is passed on with a new slant and it is not long before it comes back in a bad way. Unhealthy criticism only repels people. Before you judge others, try to visualise how you would have acted if you were in the other person's position.

Getting into an argument has never helped win friends. Even if you win the argument, the chances are you will lose the confidence of the person who loses. Learn to give your opinion only when it is asked for. Even then, pass it on as an opinion only and not as authoritative advice. Even when you are certain of facts, and know that what you are saying is nothing but the truth, let the other party decide if your opinion is acceptable.

Don't be selfish or insincere. It does not take long to detect these shortcomings in any person. Nobody likes such a person. Never speak or act in a manner whereby your honour or integrity may be doubted. Even when you know defamatory facts about others, bury them rather than repeat them. Repeating them will not help matters and you may only add fuel to the fire.

While you may patiently hear the woes of those who place their confidence in you, and advise them sincerely and tactfully, learn to keep your problems to yourself. If you are moody and complain all the time, people will avoid you. Nobody likes brooding and sulking persons. Smile. And people will smile back at you. Laugh. And people will laugh with you. But when you brood or sulk, you will have only yourself for company.

Optimism is contagious. So is enthusiasm. When you adopt a positive attitude towards life, you will begin to realise how optimism and enthusiasm not only make you more productive, but also attract friends.

When you want people to think kindly of you, let them know that you care for them. By always being punctual, show that you care for their time. With simple courtesies like "thank you", "excuse me", "I beg your pardon" or "I'm sorry" in the course of normal living, you show that you care for their feelings. Although these things appear trifling, they add a special charm to life, making a person more likeable.

Just as important is the art of complimenting others for their achievements and things that are dear to them. Even the toughest of persons will open up on being praised. People cannot help liking you when you like them.

The Ethics of Winning People Over

Men try to win others over through flattery, by throwing lavish parties and showering presents. And they appear to achieve immediate success. However, such friendships do not last long, as these are based on material benefits and not on emotional bonds, which form the basis of all lasting relationships.

For a lifetime of success with people, there is no substitute to sincerity, integrity and honour. The man with a noble character, to whom truth and honesty are an integral part of living, is accepted as a responsible citizen, one who is worthy of their confidence. It is true that one cannot get immediate results with these virtues. But the people who really matter in life can always recognise these in the course of time. Relationships based on such strong foundations are always satisfying and lasting.

The ideal form of goodwill is built on thoughtfulness for others. Kindness, sympathy and understanding, together with the emotion of love, can be great pillars of strength. Goodwill so won is a joy forever. With the goodwill of the people around you, you build one of the finest forms of power that anyone can wield. Do not give in to deriving personal benefit from others by asking them for favours. Ask for favours only when there is no alternative. Favours rendered to you reduce your power in the same proportion as the rise in your power when you do others a favour. Self-sufficiency is a great power-builder. All people look up to those who are so blessed.

Dealing with People at Work

An important factor that affects one's success in a business or profession is the ability to get along with people. In every sphere of life one must deal with people – as customers, clients, critics or suppliers. However, the most important are the people who work with us. Many may be working as subordinates. Some as colleagues. A few may be seniors. Almost one-fourth of life is spent at work. Since it means working with people, in the interests of personal success, we need to understand the subject in more detail.

Subordinates: Just because a subordinate is in a lower position, and may be enjoying lesser income and benefits, do not treat him as an inferior. If he is of fair intelligence and receives encouragement and guidance, the chances are he may rise to your present position or even higher. Subordinates are human beings too. Therefore, treat them with the respect they rightly deserve.

Everyone is as eager as you to rise in life. Since the promotion of many subordinates may come about because of your recommendations, it is likely that many will offer suggestions to improve the quality and quantity of work. This is their way of gaining your approval and appreciation. Many of these suggestions may be ineffective and you might already have tried them. But do not turn down any suggestions without giving them a fair hearing. Be patient. If it will not work, explain why. Thus you will not kill the initiative of the person who might have worked so hard. When he knows that you welcome new ideas, and will accept ones that are useful, he will keep at it until he can find a method that does work.

Your success depends upon the success of subordinates working with you. To promote their productivity, tell them in clear words what you expect from them, and more important, how exactly they benefit if they become more productive. A man works more zealously for personal benefit than when the benefits go to others.

Keep the morale of workers high. Let them look up to you as their leader and not as a dictator. In dealing with separate levels of subordinates, do not directly handle those lower down the order, but do this through those who are in charge of their work. Let everyone know that no job is too small for you, and that you are capable of doing every little bit that you may ask him or her to do. See to it that their working environments are comfortable. Tell them how they can make the work interesting, and avoid monotony and fatigue.

Above all, have full confidence in them. Gradually pass on a part of your responsibilities to them. Let them take minor decisions themselves. This will give them a sense of involvement, besides reducing the pressure on you. This will also give you a chance to gauge their ability to take on more responsible assignments. Let your staff have honest facts. Once they get down to work, give them the encouragement, appreciation and praise they are worthy of. If things go astray, as they will sometimes, do not hesitate to support their actions before colleagues and superiors.

Men who do a good job will sometimes make mistakes. Accept these as a normal part of work and not as a deliberate act. Even when you know that the hurdle could have been avoided if the worker was extra careful, simply explain the shortcomings to him. This way he will continue to place his confidence in you and accept you as a leader.

You could, as many do, threaten such a worker with dire consequences. However, these threats can rarely be carried out. Likewise, do not promise your subordinates what you cannot deliver. Having to swallow one's threats and promises can be humiliating for any self-respecting person and you also lose the confidence of an otherwise good worker.

One cannot overemphasise the need to be fair with all subordinates. Be fair about the distribution of work, about discipline and about promotions. These things can cause great resentment. You need to have a wide outlook to handle complaints and breakdown of discipline. Be understanding, but firm. Explain your decision in clear words, leaving no scope for doubt that you may have double standards for dealing with different workers.

Let everyone enjoy your confidence and place his or

her unstinted faith in you. Do not demand respect from them. Instead, win it through your work.

Colleagues: Once you have reached a certain position in your work, dealing with colleagues who may have similar responsibilities should not present any problems. If each one of you works independently, there will not be much to bother about. The best you can do is to be cordial, friendly and helpful to them. You can share their interests and ascertain that there is harmony amongst all of you. However, if the work is such that it is inter-linked and the productivity of one affects the rest, you will have to be particularly careful that you do not let others down.

If you find one link of the chain weak, do not attack the person in-charge as inefficient, but try to carry him along. No amount of fretting and fuming can improve matters. Instead, you and the other colleagues will need to understand his problems, explain them to him, suggest solutions, and help him implement them.

If things still do not improve, it may be all right to bring the matter to the notice of the senior management. However, the chances are that seeing the results, they will already be aware of the situation.

In dealing with colleagues, do not try to exhibit your superior intelligence or ability. You may be better, but nobody likes to consider others superior. Rather than being helpful, they may try to pull you down in one of your weaker moments.

You should try to do the best you can for your team. If you are truly capable, it should not be long before the senior management spots your ability. They will move you a step ahead of others. Again, do not boast of your ability.

Senior Management: Keep the senior officials happy, not only because you need to assure them that you are capable of doing your duty well, but also since your future promotions depend upon their favourable approval. A few always try to seek an entry to the next promotion through the back door. They may use unethical methods like flattering the persons concerned, or by doing them certain out-of-the-way favours. Such methods please only an unscrupulous few. In any organisation, production and profits are the main considerations. No worker can justify his work without these.

It can be a great pleasure to work with the senior management. There is a lot one can learn from them. To please them, besides exhibiting the ability to shoulder the responsibility of doing the job well, one needs to understand their expectations. They are constantly aware of the need for increasing production and profits, and expect every worker to fulfil this responsibility. They are aware of the fact that in any work there will be problems, shortcomings and even some failures. However, they expect that a responsible person will recognise the cause for such failings and be able to find reasonable solutions. Mistakes should not be repeated. Instead, each mistake should pave the way for flawless working.

A quality common to many senior management staff is that they have a great understanding of human problems. They are quick to gain the confidence of the people they work with. Sometimes one may have to work with a person who is not very easy to deal with. He may be worthy of the position he holds. No senior executive can maintain his position until he is capable of it. The problem may be that while he may understand his specialised subject very well, he may not understand human nature in the same way.

If you come across such a person, despite the hardship it may mean to you, you will have to deal with him amiably.

You may be fair and patient with your subordinates, and may understand and appreciate their problems, but if your immediate superior does not understand your problems, don't let it discourage you. Even when a superior launches a tirade against you, do not answer back or crib behind his back. Instead, try to understand what he desires and why. If you have failed to perform well, try to analyse the shortcomings and tell him about it. Tact and patience can be your most useful tools under such circumstances.

When the management approves of your efforts, do not take the entire credit for the success. Let the entire staff share it. Your modesty will pay dividends. Be subtle about praising your own efforts. When there has been a failure, step forward and take the responsibility for it. Ensure that it does not repeat itself. Nobody likes a person who thinks he is perfect and blames others for shortcomings. Act reasonably. And you will be accepted for what you really are.

The quality most appreciated by the senior management is how eager a person is to improve his past performances. If you can do a little more than what is expected of you, you make it known that you are capable of shouldering more responsibility – a hallmark of all senior men. The ability to be able to analyse past failures, and to profit by the knowledge, is another quality that will promote you to higher positions in life.

Dealing with Joblessness and Layoffs

Everyone must remember one truth. If anything can go wrong, it will! As one sets out in life to reach greater heights, he will reach there.

However, it does happen sometimes that for reasons beyond his control, he may lose his job. There may be a slowdown in the business and industry. His department

125

may become redundant and unnecessary. The company may close down. There may be a merger, necessitating some layoffs. There may be a major change in the company's management. The company may decide to hire younger people who infuse enthusiasm, fresh ideas and new ways to develop business. It can be a serious setback to any person who has a family to support.

How should one react under such circumstances? With liberalisation of trade and industry all over the world, there is a major change in the attitude of managements. More than ever before, all business and professional activity revolves around two factors – productivity and profits. Everyone must be conscious of this fact. Changes strike very rarely like lightning. They brew gradually over a long period. One should be able to sense them long before they become a reality. He should never be taken unawares.

A major casualty of losing a job is one's self-esteem. This is related to one's self-confidence. Therefore, it is important that one should not take the situation as one would a calamity. It is only a temporary setback. If one were careful, it might not have happened. If it has struck, it will pass away.

This situation should not be allowed to affect relationships within the family, with friends and others. Under no circumstances should one be disgruntled or de-motivated. This is the time to act and put one's experience to use.

Every person needs to be well informed about employment trends in one's line of work, the company one works for and also about competitors, both within the country and abroad. The complete man should stay a step ahead and forever be on the lookout for opportunities where his skills and talents could be best utilised. It would be ideal to keep in touch with prospective employers.

Even when that is not possible, one must have the details readily available so that one can move from one position to another.

To avoid a situation where one loses his job, one should be particularly careful in gradually making oneself indispensable. This is not easy. Neither is it impossible. To make it possible, one needs to be in harmony with the culture of the company, be a person who knows how to handle problems. If one is forever improving upon his managerial and technological skills, can communicate well, and works as a leader guiding a team, employers will think several times before declaring his position redundant.

Upgrade Your Skills Regularly

Wherever you are living, make a note of as many top professionals that you know of. Where were they five years ago? Ten years ago? Are they enjoying the same position as they did earlier? Or are they better off today?

You will have two types of people, those who are stagnating, and a few who are on their way up. When you observe both the categories closely, you will notice that the difference lies in their attitude towards upgrading their skills regularly.

Stop reading the newspaper for ten days. When you meet your friends at the end of this period, you will find you are not well informed. Similarly, when you fail to upgrade your skills on a regular basis, you are making your services uncompetitive. No professional can afford to do this. Certainly not the complete man!

After a certain period of growth, a person stops growing physically. However, the same person starts learning soon after birth, as he becomes conscious of this world and continues to learn and grow in the field of knowledge and skills until death, or until whatever stage he chooses to.

If one fails to upgrade skills and professional knowledge, mid-career obsolescence is sure to strike. There are younger people waiting to take over. Knowledge in every field is growing very rapidly. If one were to ignore it, one would become obsolete. Only a few years ago, computers were a luxury for a few companies. When computerisation came, those with an open mind adopted and learnt this new skill to put their experience to better use. Younger people overtook those who scoffed at it.

Being aware of the necessity of upgrading one's skills on a regular basis, all companies now have a human resources development department. Even those companies that cannot afford to have a specialised department avail of facilities offered part-time by individuals and groups involved in this activity. To ensure one does not become redundant, one must avail of these facilities when an opportunity arises.

When not available through one's company, one can still upgrade skills through additional part-time study at an institution or even through a correspondence course. Many leading business schools offer courses for working executives. Magazines and books pertaining to one's subject continue to be important sources of knowledge. Several sites on the Internet provide valuable information. Attending seminars for specialised knowledge can be expensive, but one could persuade one's company to sponsor the same.

Dealing with People in Daily Life

One also needs to deal with people in other spheres of life. A genial temperament is an asset when dealing with people whom you may or may not meet again in daily life. Daily, we come in contact with many people – salesmen, taxi drivers, the staff at hotels and restaurants, the lift attendant, and even our own domestic staff. The person who gets the best service is the one who radiates happiness and goodwill.

Do not look down upon those who serve you. Instead, make it a point to thank them every time they serve you. Be particularly gracious when a special favour is done to you, however small it may be. It may be small from your point of view, but not from that of the person serving you. Appreciation always promotes better service the next time.

Communicating with People

You may be the most intelligent person in the world, but if you cannot communicate your thoughts effectively, your ability is as good as nothing. Even a person of average intelligence has comparatively better chances of success in his dealings if he can communicate his thoughts effectively.

Normally, one needs to communicate either through speech or writing. When the audience is rather huge it will become necessary to communicate on a larger scale, which may be in the form of public speaking, or if it is in writing, through well-worded circulars and letters.

Although most people assert that they communicate very clearly, experience shows that the results are often far from satisfactory. There are several reasons for this. When a person conveys a message, it is assumed that the person receiving it has a certain amount of intelligence to receive it in the correct perspective. But intelligence and understanding vary significantly from person to person. Therefore, different people may interpret the same message in different ways.

Most people are poor listeners and their minds drift elsewhere even when they appear to be listening carefully. It is also likely that the person may fail to register the message when it is conveyed to him. This is also true of written messages. Although no person can claim not to have got the complete message, most people may read messages inattentively and are likely to miss important points, defeating the very purpose of the communication.

This places an important responsibility on the person conveying the message. For a communication to be effective, make it as clear and interesting as you can. Explain what is to be done. By whom? Why? When? Where? How? If it is a verbal message, do not forget that it is not only the flow of words that matter, but also the tone and pitch of the voice. All these can make the message effective or ineffective. After you have conveyed it, do check whether it has been properly understood.

In conveying a written message, write just as you would speak. Do not be pedantic. Too many people become unduly conscious of putting their thoughts on paper, and somehow turn too stiff to permit the normal flow of thoughts. Using simple language, keep the message short and to the point. All that is necessary is that the message should convey what is intended. If your message is in the form of a letter, use the best paper, a neat letterhead, and have it correctly typewritten. Besides the message, a letter conveys the personality of the writer, and you will do well to make your letter a fair representation of yourself. Make it pleasantly attractive, interesting and clear and it will produce the desired results.

Most people make reports and circulars too drab and uninteresting to attract the attention of the reader. Make them attractive, simple and short. In wording them, put your imagination to work to arouse the interest of the person reading it. Word the opening sentence intelligently to attract immediate attention. Follow it with the message in as few words as possible to make the meaning clear and understandable. Initially, this may appear difficult. But once you learn it, you can be certain of greater efficiency and better results. Perhaps the most difficult form of communication for the average person is speaking to a big gathering. Even otherwise capable persons find it most unnerving. Their thoughts freeze the moment they face an audience. Yet, this is one of the finest virtues one can develop. It helps build self-confidence and promote oneself in business or public life. To master this art, learn the basics and practise them as often as you can.

Initially, if you do not wish to take the risk of going onstage as the chief speaker, speak for a short while in the course of a discussion. This will help you overcome stage fright and gain self-confidence. As soon as you muster enough courage, select an occasion when you can address a small audience in the office or the club.

Speak on your favourite subject. But you will have to select the subject in keeping with the audience's taste if you want to be a successful speaker. Make certain that you are fully prepared. Any audience can be rather demanding. If the subject matter does not interest them, it is not long before they become very fidgety. The disturbance can put off many a good speaker.

A speech should be written beforehand even if you would not like to carry it with you. Do not memorise it word for word. Do read it as often as you can until you remember the keywords and phrases, which you may like to use to emphasise your points. Once you have grasped the points fully, note them in the correct sequence on a small card or paper that you can conveniently carry and consult during the actual speech. As you go through the speech repeatedly during your private rehearsals, you can polish it for the desired effect.

In finalising your speech, remember one very important point. The purpose of your speech is to convey a message to the audience in a given period of time. You can do it only if you know your subject well enough to keep it within the time allotted. Do not make time an excuse for bad preparation. The audience is never interested in excuses and apologies. These can irritate them. The people have assembled to hear your message, and the more convincingly you deliver it, the better will it be received.

Even the dullest of subjects can be made interesting with a little imagination. If you want the audience to be on your side, tell them how your message can benefit them. Your opening remarks should draw immediate attention. Follow it with the main speech point by point. Avoid repetitions. The moment you feel that you have said what you want, conclude the speech and return to your seat.

Do not let the delivery of the speech frighten you. Dress befittingly for the occasion. When you speak, the eyes of the entire audience will be on you. First impressions are important. The very fact that you have been asked to address an audience means that you can deliver an important message to them. Use the knowledge of this personal superiority over the audience to bolster your self-confidence. As you stand up to speak, smile, control your voice and open the speech. These initial moments are the most crucial. Once you can gain control over yourself, you can deliver your speech looking the audience in the eye.

This confidence grows with practice and experience. Once you have gained it, do not misuse it by speaking indefinitely. Do not make a speech longer than necessary. It may ruin the very purpose of the speech. The message completed, allow some time for questions and then return to your seat. If you have infused some of your enthusiasm into the audience, promoted their knowledge about your subject and left them with a desire to hear more, you have done well.

The Art of Changing People

It takes all types to make this world. Everyone grows up with certain thoughts about what is right and what is not. While there are many who would like to convert others to their way of thinking, not many are willing to change. With their negative attitudes towards life, a vast majority see no benefit in changing their way of life. It is for this reason that most people who set out to change others find their efforts have been in vain.

On the other hand, if a person sets out to change his

own attitudes to accept people as they are, he begins to find the world a more agreeable and happy place to live in.

When some people are willing to change, it is only because they find there is some benefit in it for them. The desire to change may be aroused when a person can identify himself with another who is very much like him, and has attained what he had desired.

Never demand that another person must change. Ensure that you use the right tools – tact and patience. These abilities single out the man who gets along well with people and can be easily cultivated by anyone willing to make the effort.

Finding Happiness

It is a personal challenge for the complete man to be able to get along well with people. People are a source of joy for those who can understand them. Through this understanding, one can be successful at home, in business, or in society.

However, do not let this get you over-entangled with pleasing people. Some people get involved to extreme limits. Their personal happiness is sacrificed in the process of following other people's wishes. These people live not for their own happiness, but for that of those people who are not capable of managing their own lives, thus creating chaos in everyday life.

Nobody can please everyone all the time. Enjoy a balanced life that has a place for friends and companions, but not at the cost of personal freedom and happiness. Be with people to enjoy the relationship, yet stay aloof to enjoy privacy. It is for you to keep your relationship with people congenial and satisfying.

Points to Ponder
- ❖ One must learn how to get along well with others.
- ❖ People cause stress. Have the right type of people

around you.

- ❖ Harmony in personal relationships can increase personal power.
- ❖ Understand people. Leadership depends upon it.
- ❖ Never overlook ethics in winning people over.
- ❖ Work exposes one to people at all levels.
- ❖ Pre-empt layoffs by upgrading your skills regularly.
- ❖ Thoughtfulness makes relationships comfortable.
- ❖ Effective communication helps in influencing people.
- ❖ Do not try to change people.
- ❖ Good relationships promote happiness.

■ ■

3. The Role of Money

"It's good to have money and the things that money can buy, but it's good, too, to check up once in a while and make sure that you haven't lost the things that money can't buy."

–George Horace Lorimer

Money plays an important role in everyday life. We spend a considerable amount of time to earn it, and then use it to buy necessities for the family and ourselves, to satisfy our many desires and, in general, to promote ourselves in society.

Each of us feels that we can do a lot better if we have a little more money. However, most of us have to be content with what we can earn. We regulate our expenses in proportion to our salaries. Even those in business and trade keep their expenses within limits, as even in the most steady of trades there are lean periods, just as there are boom periods.

Personal finances affect our peace of mind. If things are not too happy, there is a detrimental effect on our health and mental stability. To avoid these hurdles, we need to understand the true worth of money and learn how to earn it to our maximum ability. Finally, we need to use it in the most intelligent manner to make the best of it, finding contentment and satisfaction for the family and us.

One cannot overlook the need for savings either. Our future security depends upon it. We need to make money a useful servant, not a master.

The Influence of Money

Money has many advantages. Therefore, it is natural for everyone to desire and work for it. The desire for it has motivated men to great heights of sacrifice. However, it has also driven many to the lowest ways of life.

Money is capable of doing much good for society. Put to correct use, it brings progress and prosperity. But the good that money can do is limited to the ability and intelligence of the persons who use it. Money puts all people on trial. To gain a profit is natural and right, as long as it represents the value of labour of a person.

Yet some want to attain it out of proportion to their efforts. They want it through any means. It is not long before they begin to realise that to gain it at the cost of one's conscience is a heavy price. Excess money can corrupt one. Money for its own sake gives very little satisfaction, if any at all. Everyone has a limited span of life. If money cannot be put to good use in one's lifetime, of what good would it be to any person? The only justifiable reason to own it should be for the good it can do.

Savings should form a part of daily living. An honest way to earn and a benevolent outlook towards spending it is the only intelligent way of handling money.

How Rich are You?

What is it that makes one man rich and another poor? Is it the amount of money each possesses? Worldly possessions? Or their personal needs and circumstances? If it is money that makes one rich, how much does one require to be truly rich?

It is not easy to answer these pertinent questions precisely, as the word 'rich' means different things to various people. The needs of people at different levels in society are variable and so is their concept of what it takes to make a person rich. While Rs 1,000 may be a lot of money for some, even Rs 10,000 may be paltry for others.

You are as rich as you think you are. It is not the money you possess that decides how rich you are, but your mental outlook about it. A man is rich when he can fulfil his needs within his means, and can yet have something left over to carry forward for the future. To be rich means to be able to satisfy one's wants confidently. It can also mean the ability to control one's wants. This is important. Man's needs are unlimited. If one were to satisfy each one of them, no amount can be enough. Therefore, the greatest of all riches lies in the ability to exercise control over one's desires. It is a never-failing power that is a part of oneself.

The virtuous are always rich. They count on their abilities rather than money. Great riches lie in being educated, honest and straightforward. Once the needs of a home and the basic necessities are fulfilled, the virtuous work not just for the money they need for fulfilling their other needs, but also to contribute their mite towards making a better world. As a reward, they get the extra money that comes naturally in the process.

These people seek contentment through service to others through their vocations. Society accepts them as rich not for the money they possess, but because they can pay their debts of living honourably. When a man endowed with humane qualities uses his personal abilities for the maximum benefit of as many people as possible, the people around him naturally accept him.

Towards Greater Riches

To move towards greater riches, two aspects must be understood. Firstly, the need to develop a reasonable control over one's desires and, secondly, the ability to earn more money than what is immediately required to satisfy one's desires.

Since each one of us is the master of his own will, it is sheer pretence to claim that we cannot control our desires. When one has succeeded in satisfying reasonable needs for a comfortable home, security and a respectable place in society, it should not be difficult to curb other desires intelligently. To some degree, it is good to desire material pleasures. These desires stimulate one into action and hard work. One's happiness is related to the level of contentment one enjoys in life. If we are not willing to strike a reasonable balance between our desires and our capacity to fulfil them, it will only be at the cost of our personal happiness. To develop greater personal power, one must learn to live as simply as practical.

Another important step towards greater riches is to develop an intelligent attitude towards money. Many men are acclaimed rich not because they have a lot of money, but because they appear to be so. These men have developed the confidence peculiar to the rich. Such confidence is natural when more money is owed to you, rather than owed by you. Nobody keeps money at home. It is invested either in business, stock, securities or perhaps as cash in the bank. In each case, it means that money is owed to you. To exhibit the confidence of owning it, one does not need to draw on it. One only needs to enjoy the mental pleasure of possessing it in some form.

The mental satisfaction that you can draw upon gives great confidence. Those who have been able to balance their income and expenses can also develop this confidence. When a person can couple this with added goodwill of friends and others, giving him the feeling that he can always draw upon it in case of need, the confidence he develops may be all the more significant. It is certainly not hypocrisy. It is power. It can surely add new dimensions to one's living.

The second aspect towards attaining greater riches is

the ability to earn more money to satisfy more desires. This aspect receives greater attention from most people. The desire for money spurs people to great action. Unfortunately, most efforts are misdirected and the percentage of successful people is small. Few realise that success comes only from organised effort.

There are two ways of getting more money – through hard work or by making a fast buck. The latter promises fast returns, but not without the risk of personal humiliation and punishment. This is only for those who have lost their conscience and character. Do not be misled by those who are deceptively rich. One can possess other people's money and enjoy life with it, deceiving others with an impression of being rich.

Increasing Personal Earning Capacity

If we make an organised effort in the correct direction, we can substantially increase our earning capacity. For this, we must either take up a job that is more paying, or we must be willing to offer more labour by way of working longer. In each case, a certain amount of time and responsibility is involved. If we genuinely desire more money, we should be willing to offer more work.

To promote oneself to a better paid job there is the constant need for self-improvement, better work turnover, and willingness to shoulder more responsibility. The man on his way up develops a vision to recognise opportunities that come his way. He has the ability to make the best of each of them. Competition in life is a personal challenge for him. He is not afraid to change his job to a more progressive unit.

For several reasons, many are not willing to risk a changeover to jobs that are more competitive. They may have reached a slab of income where they are content. As they look at the few annual increments due to them, or the uncertain bonus that their company may offer, they may feel that they could do with a little extra money earned through a part-time job or through some special service they may be able to offer. This will, of course, mean lesser leisure time, more physical strain, and may mean more time away from home. All these will require fair adjustments to be made and exercised well ahead of time. Under such circumstances, personal experience can be a valuable asset.

One can take up a part-time job in a line with which one is already well acquainted. There are many instances when men have been able to supplement their income by starting a small industry in the garage. In such cases, family cooperation and a suitable local market can be useful assets.

Many more have added handsomely to their incomes through hobbies like writing, photography, electronics, etc. This way they have been able to combine pleasure and work. Yet, others have started small-scale business concerns where they have undertaken to sell items by post. Exporting indigenous wares to faraway countries offers a fascinating opportunity to get in touch with people abroad and earn profitable returns. The scope of starting a small part-time business is immense, and one adapts the business to suit personal aptitude and convenience.

A stage may come when one is confronted with another question. Till what point should one continue to raise earnings? Once a person has satisfied certain human needs, and learnt to earn enough money in the process, he is tempted to continue to increase his inputs to raise the income. But one needs to remember that money is capable of doing both good and bad. In excess, it can make a person proud and arrogant and rob him of the strength of his character, of ethics, and affect his health – none of which money can buy. This is where one needs to draw the line.

Of course, the word 'excess' will denote different amounts for different people. However, we can safely call that amount excess when a person feels that in working for it, he is standing at the brink of losing what he cannot buy with his money. Each individual is his own judge. He will do well to stop before it is too late.

Getting the Best with Money

To assure financial satisfaction you must follow a definite system to spend your money. The majority spend as and when the need arises. This simple system might have worked quite satisfactorily so far, but it has many pitfalls. To get the best out of your money, you will need to allow a place for everything. To enable you and the family to derive more pleasure out of the money you spend, you will need to have a plan. The little effort involved will be well rewarded.

Your first concern should be household expenses. You can allocate a reasonable amount for this in consultation with your wife. And both must strive to keep the household expenses within this limit.

Like household expenses, the payment of taxes cannot be avoided. If you are in service, your income tax will be deducted at source, although you will still have the responsibility of filing returns. If self-employed, you are supposed to deposit your taxes in time. Penalties for delayed or non-payment of taxes can be severe. Some states enforce taxes like profession tax, and you will do well to update your knowledge by consulting a tax expert from time to time. Taxes like house tax, water tax, conservancy tax, etc are best included as a part of household expenses.

Savings must form an important part of your monthly earnings. Some women save separately out of the household expenses, but that should not deter the husband from saving independently. Many people save through their contribution to the provident fund, life insurance or other schemes, but a part of it must be in the form of cash deposited in the bank or post office savings account.

Finally, we come to personal expenses. Some feel that since they are the bread-earners of the family, they have the right to spend as much as they like. One need not skip on the essentials, or on certain pleasures like smoking or an occasional outing with friends, but moderation is important. Allocate a reasonable sum for your personal expenses each month. Keep within this limit. Do inform your wife so that she does not feel she is being cheated.

You can spend the amount on your hobbies, friends, or whatever pleases you, provided you do not cross the limit you have imposed upon yourself. If you cross the barrier once, you will do it a hundred times. In addition, each time it will become more difficult to get over the temptation of doing it again. Your money will fail to buy what it should, and you will have little chance of finding financial satisfaction.

Keeping Track of Money

Somehow, most people are too lazy to keep track of their money through proper records. Each time their money is spent, they wonder where it went! This can be very distressing.

Accounts can be revealing and can tell from where the money comes, when and where it goes. They indicate amounts spent on unnecessary items or on essentials. For such accounting, you need not be proficient in professional accounting methods. Simple accounts written in an ordinary pocket diary are enough. You must be regular, though.

You will do well to simultaneously maintain a file in which you can keep bills, cash memos, receipts and other documents for future reference. You may require them to claim faulty manufacture of goods, or in case a payment is wrongly claimed twice. Receipts for payment of taxes, house rent, electricity and water bills are important papers that can be required at a future date. Therefore, they must be maintained at least for a few years from the date of issue.

Money and Honesty

Money offers the greatest temptation to be dishonest. With it one can buy not only the necessities of life, but also some of the finest luxuries and pleasures life can offer, many of these being status symbols. People can be dishonest with money in many ways. Those who feel might is right may like to steal it; those with more brains than brawn may get it through fraud. Many sophisticated thieves cheat the government by evading taxes on the pretext that it is their hard-earned money. If they are not passing this to the government, it is all right.

In addition, many may be cleverly cheating their friends and others by using borrowed money without the intention of returning it. One can draw a long list of ways by which people cheat.

However clever one may seem, no negative action goes unpunished. Since all actions continue to affect a person's personality, even the most secret dealings take their toll. Eventually, the end result will be there for everyone to see. Which is why all religions, philosophers and seers have repeatedly emphasised that honesty is the best policy. As with all other things, this is true with money also.

The Problem of Taxes

We may not like taxes, but we have to pay them. So there is no use fretting, fuming and losing sleep over this. We need to arrange our affairs to set a fair balance between demand and our willingness to pay. We can always plan to pay the least possible amount.

Tax evasion offers a ready temptation to everyone, but it is illegal. Once caught, there can be serious consequences. However, one can take advantage of the many concessions allowed in certain cases. This way one can legally avoid excessive taxation. There are many avenues that one can take advantage of. Many utilities offer rebate on timely payment of bills. For income tax, one can claim several concessions on the use of a bicycle, scooter or car for professional use. Even on purchase of books and magazines, on incomes from agriculture, dairy or poultry, or on interest from the post office savings bank, or a scheduled bank.

In the same way, you can avail of tax savings on life insurance premium, health insurance, medical care of dependants and the like. Charities to certain institutions also enjoy tax concessions. For purposes of wealth tax too, many exemptions are available.

The above list of concessions is not exhaustive. The rules keep changing yearly. If one can keep in touch with a good tax adviser, the benefits of such concessions can be availed of to pay less.

Savings

One cannot achieve financial satisfaction unless a certain amount of money is set aside regularly as savings. Most people contend that they do not earn enough to save. This is mostly an excuse for their bad habit of not saving. In many cases, a part of the salary is deducted at source as provident fund, life insurance premium or other forms of saving. It is most essential that some money be set aside as cash also.

One should not wait until the end of the month to see what is left from the salary to save. Instead, a part of the monthly income must be set aside first thing every month when the amount is distributed for expenses under the various heads. Some money must be set aside as cash savings in a bank.

Investing the Savings

Many people have saved huge sums throughout their life and then suddenly lost it by investing this with an unscrupulous person or business concern. Such losses can adversely affect a person's mind and health. As you save, you also need to learn how to be a shrewd investor. The security of your savings is important not only for you, but also for your family. The more secure your savings, the better the security you and your family will enjoy in life.

The chief criterion while investing your savings should be that your money must be available to you when you need it. From this point of view, the best place to keep the money is in a bank savings account. This way it earns interest and is readily available for withdrawal in case of need. As the amount accumulates, you can shift it once a year to a fixed deposit in the bank. The rate of interest is higher, but you will be required to leave your amount with the bank for a fixed period. However, if you need this money before the end of the stipulated period, you can normally withdraw it in the form of a loan from your bank with the deposit as security.

Banks offer many other savings options like a cumulative deposit scheme, public provident fund scheme, and various kinds of fixed deposit schemes. Post offices also offer savings bank facilities and investments in savings certificates. Several Mutual Funds offer attractive schemes. Tax concessions are available on many of these investments. You can get the details from the bank, post office or the Mutual Fund.

Investment in personal life insurance offers many advantages. While you save to collect a large sum of money at an advanced age, it offers security to your family in case of death. Life insurance policies of different kinds are available offering special features like provision for children's education or marriage, savings, and for other purposes. Any life insurance agent will be pleased to explain the details of the many policies that he can offer you. All these offer concessions in income tax. Most of them offer security in case of death. If required, loans are available with the life insurance policy as a form of security.

Many commercial concerns also accept deposits at

fixed rates of interest, besides offering their shares for sale to the public. Many progressive companies are good investment risks. The rate of interest on the deposits is fixed. On their shares, they pay an annual dividend in proportion to the profits of the company. The shares also enjoy the advantage of a rise in their value in the share market. For the average person who has little knowledge of financing and the risks involved in it, it would be safer to invest in more known forms of investment.

Investment with private businessmen can be risky unless the persons concerned are well known. In the business world, quite a few unscrupulous people are known to swindle simple investors through promises of big profits. Investments in the form of purchase of land, a house, or merchandise at special rebates should be well looked into, preferably by a lawyer, before the deal is transacted.

A Bank Account

Surprisingly, many people are still too shy to operate a bank account. Contrary to common belief, a bank does not cater to the rich only. It caters to everyone. A savings account can be opened with as little as Rs 500. If one maintains a reasonable balance, he is entitled to withdrawals by cheque. Banks offer many facilities to customers. It does not take more than a few minutes to deposit or withdraw money.

If you are in service, rather than handle cash, you can have your salary transferred directly to your bank account. If in business, you could transfer the amount allocated for household expenses to a savings account maintained for the purpose and operated by you and your wife. From here, you can pay bills by cheques, saving you the bother of handling cash each time.

Here are some tips to operate a bank account smoothly:

1. Register your specimen signature in the bank in

SECTION-IV

simple handwriting and make it a point to sign all cheques in the same manner each time.

2. Count the number of cheques when you collect a chequebook from the bank.

3. Keep your passbook and chequebook in a safe place.

4. Make all deposits with a pay-in slip, keeping the counterfoil receipt in a file.

5. As far as practical, accept and make payments by cheque.

6. Make certain that you have a sufficient balance in your account before issuing a cheque.

7. Do not overlook to fill the counterfoil of every cheque you use.

8. Cheques issued to business concerns having bank accounts must be crossed.

9. All cheques above Rs 10,000 must be crossed. The income tax authorities desire this.

10. Send your passbook to the bank for updating as often as necessary to keep the entries up-to-date.

Financial Satisfaction

Finding personal financial satisfaction is a matter of personal attitude towards money. We need money to satisfy personal needs. Since the financial satisfaction will not only depend upon one's individual needs, but also that of the wife and the family, the ultimate success depends upon creating a fair balance between family needs and resources.

External influence by way of keeping up with friends and society can also affect the satisfaction that the family derives from its resources. However, keeping up with friends and others by spending beyond one's personal resources just to maintain false family status is a game that nobody can win. The position of an individual or a family does not depend upon their financial and material possessions, but on the goodwill that they can generate in society.

Many men have accumulated large sums of money through fair and foul means. However, it never did them any good. Money is best as a servant. When made the master, it brings only displeasure and sorrow.

Points to Ponder

- ❖ Everybody needs money. The more the better.
- ❖ Understand money. It is a force for both good and bad.
- ❖ Money puts everyone on trial.
- ❖ To be rich, you do not need as much money as you think.
- ❖ Put your money to the best use. Keep track of it.
- ❖ Save wisely. Pay taxes honestly.
- ❖ Maintain a bank account.
- ❖ Aim for financial satisfaction. It will keep you happy.

■■

4. Living Efficiently

"It is more than probable that the average man could, with no injury to his health, increase his efficiency 50 per cent."

–Walter Dill Scott

The only way to meet the challenge of today's modern, highly competitive society is to accept the concept of efficiency in everyday life. Efficiency experts have invaded almost every sphere of life. Be it the home, the workplace or our social life, there always is a better and easier way to do what we are presently doing in our daily routine.

What is Efficiency?

Some people have a knack of living almost effortlessly. Even after a full day's work, they do not show the slightest signs of boredom or fatigue. They are able to provide satisfying companionship to the family as tirelessly as they cope with a range of other activities. They have time for extra-curricular activities and some more to spare to participate in social life. These people find happiness in everything they do. Their secret is rather simple – they are just plain efficient.

To be efficient means to be competitive and to be able to effectively meet the needs of the day. It means to be able to achieve more in less time or with lesser effort and without any strain on personal health or leisure. It means to find contentment and happiness in everything one needs to do.

Increasing Personal Efficiency

Each one of us is capable of increasing our efficiency manifold. This can be achieved in two ways. Firstly, we need to understand how we can use the wonderful power gifted to us by nature. Secondly, we must ascertain that none of this power is wasted through wrong and unnecessary actions. Nature has endowed everyone with this vital power, but unfortunately few recognise it or put it to good use.

To begin with, become conscious of this vital force within you. It can transform you into an altogether new person. The first requisite to develop this power is good health. You must learn to be healthy if you want to be efficient. Even if not blessed with perfect health, you can still make the best of it by learning to live with your limitations. It is your attitude towards health that will take you a long way towards more efficient living.

If your present habits are holding you back from moving ahead, perhaps you need to do some self-evaluation of your activities. Is your routine well planned? Is it free from petty annoyances, allowing you to concentrate on your main objectives? Is your time well utilised? Are you able to reasonably achieve the targets for the day set by you? Alternatively, is it that you do no advance planning at all and rely upon an alibi each time you fail to score your marks? These simple pointers can provide a lot of food for thought. If you use this knowledge in your daily living, you can increase your productivity to personal advantage.

One can draw a lot of strength from self-discipline. Learn to control your emotions. Do not waste your energy on negative emotions like anger, jealousy, hatred or revenge. Instead, develop a wider and more positive attitude towards life. Conserve as much energy as you can so that it can be utilised for purposes that are more useful. Speak less. A lot of energy is wasted on unnecessary speech. Make self-education a continuous process. Be on the lookout for improvements you can adopt in your life. This will gradually increase your self-confidence and your system will readily release more energy for use.

Do not procrastinate. What needs to be done today, must be done right away. However good an excuse you may have, to procrastinate means to make it known that you are not efficient enough to cope with your daily work. In the same way, do not postpone making decisions that need to be made as a part of daily routine. Do think twice before you make the decision, but unless you are certain that it is to your benefit, do not postpone it. It is better to make a wrong decision, and learn by it, than not to make a decision at all. Indecisiveness is the hallmark of the inefficient.

Do not let problems discourage you. Worry and anxiety can sap energy and leave one confused, tired and inefficient to tackle further work. One must face defeat as one would face success and thereby conserve a lot of energy that would otherwise go waste. There is no one in the world who does not have his share of problems. However, the efficient man knows that there is a solution to every problem. It can always be found, provided one is eager to find it. Nobody is defeated unless he gives in and lets people know about it. Therefore, keep up the struggle. Perseverance always brings success. It adds to one's self-confidence.

One of the most important factors affecting personal efficiency is the inability of the majority to cope with the tensions of daily life. When these tensions cannot be regularly and intelligently released, the outcome is fatigue. If fatigue stems from the monotony of doing the same thing continuously, try your hand at different kinds of work for a change. If it comes from overwork, take rest. The most important aspect of this problem is that you must understand the pattern of fatigue you suffer from. Avoid causes that promote it. Initially, you may not be able to pinpoint the exact causes, but as you become conscious of this problem, you can eliminate them one by one. As a rule, arrange an interesting work schedule with brief periods of rest in between. Balance work and pleasure in the daily routine.

Finally, do not overlook the need for good sleep. It is nature's way of giving you renewed strength for meeting the challenge of yet another day.

Get Organised for Efficient Living

As one learns to draw on the vast storehouse of energy, one should use it in organising an efficient daily routine.

Your home is your retreat from the problems of the outside world. At the same time, it is your springboard to jump to greater achievements and recognition in your work and in society. It is therefore important that if you want to be free to tackle important issues outside the home, the co-operation of your wife and family should be assured. They can substantially contribute to your success by ensuring harmony inside the home.

Plan your activities. Plan for the next few months, for the weeks to come and for the day you are setting out for in the morning. Work out priorities. Fix the time by which each task must be done. In the beginning, you may not be able to forecast your schedule accurately and from time to time some changes may have to be incorporated. However, with growing experience you will begin to realise the advantage of working to a system.

Allocate a time for everything in your work schedule. For reading, correspondence, dictating letters, delegating work to subordinates, meeting visitors, working out improvements, conferring with seniors and other such matters that may require your attention everyday. However, have some flexibility in your routine to allow you to attend to more pressing needs sometimes. This will not disturb your work output in case of emergencies.

When at work, do not let side issues or interruptions distract you; tackle one thing at a time. If you try to do many things at the same time, the results will be confusing. Besides, confusion can sap a lot of energy.

Teach your subordinates to be self-sufficient to allow you more time to tackle the important problems. Teach them how to communicate effectively. If they come to you with a problem, let them bring a complete analysis of the same and a possible solution if they have one to suggest. This way they will solve many problems on their own and all that they may require from you is a go-ahead signal, saving much of your time in the process.

An efficient secretary can be a great asset. She could record and reply to telephone calls, go through the preliminary details before sending in a visitor to meet you, handle routine correspondence and attend to several similar details everyday.

In any sphere of activity, communications and papers of all descriptions play an important part. Organise an efficient system of keeping important papers filed. Ensure that you get a paper when you want it.

Most important of all, keep your work interesting. Do not let monotony set in because this will promote fatigue. Alternate between different kinds of work. This keeps the mind alert. Avail of brief periods of rest particularly when there is a rush of work. Although tension builds up faster during fast work, rest soon relieves it.

One derives great satisfaction and strength from orderly work. If you want your efficiency to grow daily, ensure no work is left on your table each evening. If something needs to be postponed for some reason, do not place it in the cold storage. At the end of each week, review all pending matters. Once a month follow this with a thorough check-up of your desk drawers for anything you might have inadvertently tucked away.

Do not look forward to the end of the day as yet another day done with. Be enthusiastic about the success achieved that day. Look forward to the wonderful evening that lies ahead to be spent with your wife and family. This can be the best time of the day if you make it so intelligently. Do not take any work home. The chances are that after a full day at it you will not be able to tackle it efficiently. Furthermore, even if you make a heroic effort to get over it, you may have done one job, but you will have many other problems in return.

The evening is a time to do things you like best. Take your family to a movie or to the club, watch television or listen to your favourite music, visit friends, take some time off for your hobbies or just have a quiet time with the family. Such activities help release tension built up during the day. Take full advantage of relaxation; look forward to a peaceful night's sleep and yet another wonderful day ahead.

Efficiency Aids

To promote personal efficiency, take advantage of every efficiency aid you can use. There are many available in the market, but mostly people adapt aids to personal needs. A diary in which you can record appointments, important data to be remembered, reminders to be sent, and such similar information is an aid that every person should use.

Similarly, a scribbling pad with a small pencil tied to it is a very useful aid. You could have such pads on your working table, near your telephone at home, in your bedroom or in any other place where you think you could benefit from it.

Another efficiency aid is an address book where you can list the names, addresses and telephone numbers of business associates, friends and others. It is an ideal place to locate names and addresses whenever you might require them. Some prefer to maintain a list of birthdays and wedding anniversaries to facilitate the sending of greetings in time.

If your business or profession requires it, you could maintain a bigger version of an address book by having a classified mailing list. However, it is important to revise the address book or the mailing lists from time to time to keep them up to date.

Visiting cards, trays to accommodate papers and files that are coming to you or going out, ball pens and pencils of varying colours to mark correspondence and documents, an intercom phone and a whole lot of similar items are used to promote efficiency. Adapt them to suit your own needs.

A personal computer is the finest aid that has changed the way people work or think. It has helped do things that were unimaginable a few years ago. All offices are equipped with them. Every progressive home has one. Put them to the best use to live more efficiently.

Always keep on the lookout for ideas you can use to promote personal efficiency.

Relaxation and Efficiency

Create a fair balance between work and rest. A very large number of people still do not understand the need for rest. Irrespective of the fact that their bodies refuse to cope with their wrong habits, they continue to place greater burden on their system, eventually paying a heavy price.

We are capable of doing various kinds of work through our muscles, which contract or relax, depending upon the need. The longer we put them to work, the longer they remain contracted. This, in turn, causes tension in the adjacent nerves, and together with the wear and tear in the muscles, causes fatigue. To overcome this, people try different measures – stimulating drinks like tea, coffee, or alcoholic beverages, massage, drugs and physical rest. Although people use these measures in varying degrees, by far the best way of relieving fatigue caused by physical exertion is rest. It is not that people are unaware of this simple fact. They simply rely upon other measures. They do not understand how to rest and gain complete relief from the tensions of everyday living.

One can learn the art of physical relaxation through a conscious effort in the right direction. Its daily practice makes it a part of one's habits. In the first place, avoid as much physical strain as you can. Remember that it is more restful to walk than to stand as this gives rest to each leg one by one. Rather than stand, it is more restful to sit. Still better, it is more comfortable to lie down. To promote relaxation, the aim should be to relax the muscles and loosen the muscle contraction completely. The moment this is achieved, the nerves become less tense. Mental activity ceases automatically. Immediate relief follows.

To make natural relaxation more satisfying, locate areas that tend to get more tired and tense. Then deliberately practise relaxing them while lying in bed in an undisturbed room. Let the muscles go limp. With each progressive effort, you will find greater relief. At the same time, because of your conscious effort to relax, you will develop a special consciousness to avoid strain whenever you can.

At work, you will begin to realise the need for comfortable furniture, a pleasant atmosphere and of having a posture that places the least strain on muscles not in use. It will be helpful if you can rest a short while each day, sitting on a comfortable chair with your eyes closed and the mind temporarily at rest. Learning the art of physical relaxation will enhance mental relaxation too. It will make you much more efficient.

Fatigue

Besides physical factors, fatigue is also caused by emotional stress. Fatigue due to physical causes is immediately evident and the body reacts by demanding rest and sleep. If one can learn to have a fair balance between work and rest, physical fatigue can regularly be relieved through relaxation.

However, we need to be careful about emotional fatigue that, as the name suggests, is induced by our own emotions. It is directly controlled by the mind. Even without the least bit of exertion, this fatigue can set in, making one tired, irritable and moody. In most cases, this fatigue sets in because of wrong mental attitudes towards life. Doing repetitive work and the monotony ensuing from it can also cause emotional fatigue. Once this fatigue sets in, few people are able to cope with it intelligently. It leads them from one thing to another, but rarely are they able to rid themselves of it completely.

As an immediate measure, this type of fatigue has been effectively, though only temporarily, controlled by drugs recommended by medical practitioners. Long-range treatment consists in changing one's personal attitude about things that cause botheration. This cannot be achieved overnight. If one keeps at it and gradually gets over bad habits and attitude in the same way as one develops good habits, there is no reason why one cannot rid himself of this vexing problem.

Organise an interesting daily routine. Do things in which you find personal satisfaction. Develop a friendly attitude towards people. Above all, constantly strive to be happy yourself.

Do not ignore fatigue. In the first place, do not let it set in. The more you tire yourself, the longer it takes to gain one's original efficiency. Avoid excessive noise, movement and oppressive weather, as all these are conducive to causing fatigue. Also, avoid unnecessary speaking. This too can be very tiring. As you become conscious of the problem of fatigue, you will learn how to avoid areas of personal conflict and thereby avoid fatigue. Your efforts will be well rewarded. Fatigue not only affects personal efficiency, but can also bring about a serious setback in one's health.

Sleep

Everyone has individual sleeping habits. While some are content with only five to six hours of sleep, others may require nine to ten hours to be fully refreshed. Most find seven to eight hours sleep quite satisfying. Some claim that they sleep very little. It seems that they fulfil their quota of sleep through short naps. However, most people prefer a single stretch of sleep. With time, people work out their own sleeping needs.

Sleep is nature's greatest tranquilliser. It recharges the battery of physical and emotional well-being in each one of us. Every efficient person uses this knowledge for personal benefit. Do not try to prolong your working hours by skipping sleep. One can gradually cut down sleeping hours without any immediate harmful effects. In the end, it will not be without harm to one's health. Both anxiety and excitement can disturb sleep. Therefore, to sleep well, one needs to control one's emotions. Physical exertion and fatigue too can cause sleeplessness as the muscles and the adjacent nerves do not relax immediately. To ensure proper sleep, adopt regular habits, avoiding late nights. Use a comfortable bed.

If you cannot go off to sleep some day, do not let it make you anxious or seek relief through drugs. Instead, trace the cause. If you are emotionally upset, try to get over it. Also, avoid stimulants like alcohol, tea and coffee. Some prefer a cup of milk as a nightcap, but it is not necessary. If you can learn to relax your muscles, your mind will automatically switch off as the muscles get relaxed. You will soon enjoy restful sleep.

Points to Ponder

❖ The concept of efficiency in everyday life has become a necessity.

❖ Understand "efficiency". It is being productive without undue stress.

- ❖ Everyone can increase personal efficiency.
- ❖ Organise your life for efficient living.
- ❖ There are efficiency aids all around us. Use them.
- ❖ A fair balance between work and rest is important.
- ❖ Understand fatigue. Never let it set in.
- ❖ There is no substitute for sleep.

■ ■

IMPORTANCE OF THE COMMUNITY

No man is an island in himself. We need each other. We depend upon each other for our survival, fulfilment and growth. Every religion emphasises that we are the children of God. Therefore, we are all related to each other.

The environment in every community is such that every person tries to get ahead of the other. Each person is forever trying to convince the community that he is better than the others. He seeks appreciation. He is waiting to be praised. He seeks greater importance amongst his fellowmen. He is forever emphasising that he is different. From here begins the journey to fame and power. People adopt all kinds of methods to achieve their objective. Their choice depends upon their upbringing and on their understanding of the inner voice. We observe it every day in the world around us.

In a hurry to achieve the best a person is capable of, people often sacrifice their rest and leisure to stretch their time. It begins in a small way. A little extra time spent at work. Day by day, it grows. Rest and leisure are totally ignored. Fatigue begins to set in. A search now begins to overcome fatigue. Soon it is a vicious circle.

The complete man has definite objectives to achieve. He has no time to experiment. A clear understanding of the situation is important. He must know how he can get ahead to achieve what he has set out to do. Again, it is a matter of self-discipline. The complete man must understand his capabilities. He must recognise and overcome his weaknesses. Recharging himself with rest and leisure, he is ready for the top position.

1. Fame and Power

"Nothing, indeed, but the possession of some power can with any certainty discover what, at the bottom, is the true character of any man."

−Burke

When a man is able to satisfy the basic needs of his family, he turns his attention to achieving fame and power. This desire arises from a deep-seated human urge to be appreciated. This appreciation is not always forthcoming. Each person is engrossed in satisfying his personal needs. He is too selfish to think of others. This leads a person to adopt varied means to attract attention from others.

The desire for fame and power is a natural one. For a man to find complete fulfilment in life, it must be reasonably satisfied. This desire is capable of motivating people to extremes of activity, for both good and bad. At times, it has raised a man from nothing to greatness. On other occasions, it has made a brute of an otherwise good man. The difference is attributed to one's personal values and attitudes. The intelligent expression of this basic desire has always interested the complete man. He has constantly endeavoured to find personal satisfaction by making adjustments to be in harmony with his basic nature.

Expression of this Power

In the home, a man looks forward to being the master and guide of his family. To him the home is the most important institution. The success achieved here satisfies his desire to be appreciated. In its finer form, it promotes intelligent growth and creativity, preparing him for greater successes in the outside world.

At work, a man finds fulfilment of this desire when he receives respect from his subordinates, acceptance as an equal by colleagues and appreciation from superiors.

In the surroundings where he lives, he expects goodwill and respect from neighbours. He wants them to believe that he stands for all things that are good and honourable. He does understand that perceptions can vary. He wants to be identified with what is best and believes that his is probably the most authentic viewpoint.

Developing Power Over Others

To each man, his own needs are of utmost importance. These must be fulfilled somehow. Each person becomes selfish to attain his own ends. With limited resources, there begins a struggle to fulfil the basic needs. One strives to develop different forms of personal power to be able to have an edge over others.

This struggle is not of recent origin. It has existed since times immemorial. One perseveres to develop this power in many forms.

Let us examine some of the important ones.

Physical Strength: This is the most primitive form of power and has been used for both offensive and defensive purposes. For primitive man, might was right. The strongest ruled over the weak. In due course of time, instead of using physical strength alone, man learnt to make and use clubs, stones and contraptions for the purposes of defence and offence, but generally, might was still right.

With the growth of civilisation, man realised that might was not always right. The perception of physical strength began to change to mean good health and the ability to withstand the hardships of life. People began to object to the use of physical strength for offensive purposes.

As society became more organised, the use of physical strength for offensive or defensive purposes was delegated to the police and military forces for use in a regulated manner. Laws were enacted to restrict the use of physical strength in the manner primitive men used it. With this, man's creativity sought out other forms for the use of physical strength to fulfil his desire for power.

Man began to develop physical strength in its positive forms – in the form of good health and a physique that anyone would be proud of. To direct this wonderful driving force in man for peaceful purposes, games and competitions to exhibit physical strength and skills were devised. Boxing, wrestling, weight-lifting, javelin and the discus throw and a range of other similar sport showcased man's ingenuity in the clever use of physical strength as a source of power.

For the complete man, physical strength should mean good health and ability to face physical hardships of life in the modern age. If the exhibition of physical strength does interest him, the field of activity in the form of sports is very large. Each activity is capable of satisfying his desire for this form of power in a regulated way.

Knowledge as Power: Having seen that physical strength as a form of power had its limitations, man used knowledge to fulfil his desire for power. Knowledge can mean anything from learning a practical skill to collecting information about a particular activity, understanding the laws of nature and finding solutions to problems. It is equipping oneself with accumulated experience put on record.

During the process of living, as a man uses the knowledge passed on to him by his ancestors, he gradually adds to it. He is able to understand circumstances better. This added knowledge is not intended for the benefit of future generations. It immediately fulfils the desire for power, as a person is better equipped with it in comparison to other people. With people all over the world rushing to seek fulfilment by gaining power through knowledge in various fields, specialisation grew in every sphere of activity. This resulted in a rapid growth of knowledge, which has helped technological advancement and better living for people all over the world.

The path of knowledge is a virtuous path. The Holy Scriptures commended it. Through it, man has been able to elevate himself by making good use of the gifts of nature. It has given him a medium through which he has been able to express his creativity and find fulfilment of his personal desires.

The field of knowledge is vast. It is not necessary that to be useful all of it must be known to us. Some of it is necessary to guide our daily life, but there is a lot that need not become a part of our memory. It should be on record for use when required. Likewise, to be practically useful, different people can specialise in different subjects to avoid duplication of effort. Knowledge is ideally gained through education. To be effective, education should aim at providing knowledge that can make a person capable of using his abilities intelligently. It is not enough to be doctors, engineers, machinists or artisans. This knowledge prepares them for one field of activity only. To be more useful, they must learn to use their abilities for the benefit of mankind.

Position in Life as Power: The desire for power is a vital driving force. Even when two persons possess similar knowledge and are of similar capabilities, each one is in constant preparation to move into a position that is more conspicuous than that of the other. To achieve this, many work on specialties. Based on their work and knowledge, they qualify to occupy exclusive positions in life, thereby fulfilling the desire to wield more power than the rest.

The desire to hold high and exclusive positions in life as a means of satisfying the desire for power has induced many to work harder, to rise in his business or profession, to become the president of his club or association, or to perhaps become a municipal councillor or a state legislator. Men seek positions in all spheres of life. They want to feel important and to direct others from their superior position. They are eager that the limelight falls on them.

This urge to show-off is so great that men go to extremes to express their superiority to relatives, friends and others. People build and live in houses that are much larger than what they require. They spend huge sums of money to acquire treasures that others cannot. They ensure that they have all the status symbols such as an imported car, a television and air-conditioning in every room bedecked with collector's pieces. They leave nothing to the imagination of the other person about their status and position in life.

There are other kinds of people, like politicians, who may deliberately shun these status symbols. They may rely upon other forms of expression of personal importance, like sitting on the stage at a public meeting. They may seek an opportunity to air their learned views or to have a personal secretary to announce their arrival or to meet and screen visitors desirous of meeting them. Whatever the mode, the idea is the same – to use one's position in life to fulfil the desire for power.

It is through personal knowledge and effort only that one can reach and maintain a high position in life. The people who reach high positions in life get their share of criticism from those who fail to make it. Little do these critics realise that a man maintains the position that he deserves. If a man was to reach a high position by any other way, and is incapable of shouldering the responsibilities that are part of the high position, it is only a matter of time when he will stabilise in a position that is in harmony with his personal capabilities. Irrespective of one's position in life, both positive and negative factors play a part in the lives of all people. The level of interaction decides the position one is fit for.

Like other forms of power, if the power from one's position in life is used for the welfare of mankind, it grows. If not, negative influences reduce it proportionately.

Money as Power: One form of power that attracts immediate attention is that which comes from money. With money one can not only purchase the necessities of life, but also purchase many luxuries to make living as comfortable as possible. Besides, money can also make it possible to attract friends and others by showering them with gifts and parties and in general, by contributing to charities. Yes, money is truly a great form of power.

Money is the criterion by which a man or a nation is termed rich and powerful. Much also depends upon how money is used. By providing security of living, it promotes personal peace of mind. In the hands of good people, it is capable of doing much good. It is capable of not only providing for its master, but when it has been used to create huge public trusts, it has also helped fight hunger, disease and pestilence, and contributed substantially in reducing human suffering. Through huge enterprises, man has used money to create opportunities for work and more comfortable living for people everywhere. It has helped bring many facilities and services, which were otherwise luxuries, within the scope of use by the average family.

What limits the possibilities of money is not that it is bad in itself, but that in the hands of the wrong person, it can do great harm. Many have lost their conscience in acquiring it. The more these people acquire, the more their greed grows. Money is good to buy what it can. However, of what good is it if in the process of earning it one were to lose what it cannot buy? No amount of money can buy one his conscience, honour, health or happiness.

Possession of money may not necessarily mean that it has been personally earned. It can also mean that it has been inherited or may even have been borrowed from others. It can therefore be quite deceptive. Many people show off status symbols purchased with money that is not their own, without anyone knowing about it. Power from inherited or borrowed money is temporary and short-lived. It can have a detrimental effect on personal values and character.

Even if a person is capable of multiplying his inherited wealth, or make a fortune from nothing, it only proves one thing: he is a success as far as earning money is concerned. It does not necessarily mean that he is capable of wielding the power money adds to its master, because many times this power can be corrupting.

Human Goodwill as Power: Finally, we come to the most potent single source of power – human goodwill! It is a vital force and, when fully developed, helps exhibit man's character in its noblest form. This source of power can work wonders irrespective of whether one is rich or poor, physically strong or weak, belongs to an exclusive group of people in high positions or is one of the rest.

This form of power is developed with positive emotions directed towards others. It comprises simple things: a smile, a tear wiped off, a ray of hope planted when things appear dark. It could begin within the family and extend to friends and others. It is a simple art of liking all people.

As a man learns to be benevolent, loving, kind, sympathetic and thoughtful towards others, he does not profit alone by projecting his own personality. He also reduces human suffering wherever he goes. For men who gain power this way, it is not a temporary rise to the pedestal. This power grows slowly, but since it is based upon accepting all the positive qualities in life, with a gradual elimination of negative ones, it becomes a part of a person.

It is this power, when fully developed, which helps one to learn how to cross hurdles in a time of trial, coming as they do in everyone's life.

All religions are based on human goodwill and commend it. Saints and philosophers have praised it in many forms. The validity of this truth has been proved by the test of time. The fame of men written in stone or metal can be wiped off, but written on the human heart, it is indelible.

The Path to Fame and Power

Each day many people set out on the path to fame and power. Unfortunately, only a few make it to their destination. Depending upon individual upbringing, education and personal attitudes, men pursue one or more of the forms described to achieve power. With time and many hurdles to cross, only a few persevere until they achieve it. Each person rises to the height he is capable of maintaining and no more. Even if he can gain some temporary advantage for a short period, it is not long before he descends to the position he deserves. Whatever one may be willing to do, fame cannot be demanded. It must be won through sacrifice and perseverance. It will come to him who deserves it.

There is no shortcut to fame and power. In certain areas of life, the limelight shines more liberally than on others, as is evident in the case of film stars, TV personalities, sportsmen, writers and the like. Many aspire to gain fame quickly this way. However, most people soon realise that the glamour is superficial and temporary.

Even if some of these personalities continue to be in the limelight for long, it is not by virtue of their activity, but because their success is backed by talent and long periods of toil. Without ability, glamour fades away as rapidly as it comes. There can really be no lasting power unless it comes from within, from personal ability, faith and goodwill towards everyone. This is true in all spheres of life.

In its own way, fame can be very cruel. With the gain of power over others on the one hand, there is loss of personal freedom on the other. One becomes a slave to the high sense of responsibility, which is the price of fame. With continued thoughtfulness about others, one's personal problems fade from the scene. Others' problems make an entry. It is satisfying, but not without the loss of personal liberties.

Points to Ponder

- ❖ Fame and power are a great motivating force.
- ❖ Everyone desires appreciation and praise.
- ❖ Desire for appreciation creates the need to feel important.
- ❖ Power through physical strength is as old as mankind.
- ❖ Knowledge is power. Everyone is rushing to acquire it.
- ❖ A position in life is power. Everyone is chasing it.
- ❖ The power from money leads everyone to materialism.
- ❖ Few understand the value of human goodwill as power.
- ❖ With fame and power, there is loss of personal freedom.

■■

2. Forms of Recreation

> "*Recreation is not the highest kind of enjoyment, but in its time and place is quite as proper as prayer.*"
>
> –S.I. Prime

There are many people even in this age who think life is really a serious affair and recreation and pleasures are only for the young and the frivolous. Perhaps they do not understand the correct meaning of the word recreation. Their thinking may be based on outmoded beliefs that pleasure is food for the senses only and that anything pleasant is necessarily dirty and sinful.

Whatever such people might think, the truth is that depending upon personal temperament and values, each one of us indulges in one form of recreation or another. Nature too intends it that way. Sleep is nature's way of giving each one compulsory relaxation. All of us know what it means to be without it.

Recreation can mean many things: a diversion in normal activities, indulging in some form of play or the simple pleasure of rest and relaxation.

A certain amount of tension is constantly building within us all the time. This is irrespective of the fact whether we are occupied mentally or physically. If we can find a suitable outlet for this tension through recreation, we stay healthy. We remain unaffected by the pressure of tension on our many organs. If we ignore this tension, as most people tend to do, we may not feel it for some time. It continues to exert an unhealthy pressure on the organs until this pressure finds an outlet in the shape of an illness, which can leave one invalid for life.

Accepting recreation as a normal part of life will enable us to release the tensions of daily living in an intelligent way. It will also enable us to live a more creative life. To achieve this, recreation must offer a change from daily routine, should help release tension and thereby offer complete relaxation, followed by a feeling of well-being. The cumulative effect results in

www.ingramcontent.com/pod-product-compliance
Lightning Source LLC
Chambersburg PA
CBHW050716280326
41926CB00088B/3062